# Heritage Law and Policy

*Listed Buildings and Conservation Areas*

**Gordon Campbell**
*Solicitor*
*Mishcon de Reya*

Palladian Law Publishing Ltd

© Gordon Campbell
2001

*Published by*
Palladian Law Publishing Ltd
Beach Road
Bembridge
Isle of Wight PO35 5NQ

www.palladianlaw.com

ISBN 1 902558 27 8 ✓

Typeset by Heath Lodge Publishing Services
Printed in Great Britain by The Cromwell Press Limited

# · Contents ·

# · Preface ·

There are now approximately 500,000 Listed Buildings in England and somewhere in the region of 8,000 Conservation Areas. Listed building legislation has been in force for very many years and is a regular source of newsworthy *cause célèbres* both nationally and locally. However, this area of law, practice and policy can still prove to be a minefield for the unwary.

In practice problems tend to arise:

- where an owner or occupier wishes to carry out works within a short time scale to a building which is already listed, and,
- Where a building becomes listed unexpectedly.

New issues of law and policy are constantly evolving. All areas of public law, and the planning system in particular, are currently starting to get to grips with the implications of the Human Rights Act 1998. One of the most fiercely argued aspects of the new legislation concerns Article 6 of the European Convention on Human Rights which provides that everyone is entitled to a fair and public hearing within a reasonable time by an independent and impartial tribunal in the determination of his rights and obligations.

In the recent "Alconbury" case (*R* v *Secretary of State for the Environment, Transport and the Regions ex parte Holding & Barnes Plc et al* [2001]) the High Court held that the processes by which the Secretary of State made decisions and orders under the Town & Country Planning Act 1990, the Transport and Works Act 1992, the Highways Act 1980 and the Acquisition of Land Act 1981 were incompatible with Article 6 in that the Secretary of State was both policy-maker and decision maker. In the course of the case the Secretary of State conceded that he was not an independent and impartial tribunal.

The provisions of the Town & Country Planning (Listed Buildings and Conservation Areas) Act 1990 frequently give rise to landowners being deprived of their property rights without any manner of hearing. Whilst appeals may be lodged against many decisions such appeals lie to the Secretary of State (*i.e.* policy maker as well as the decision maker). There remains no appeal against the initial listing of a building or designation of a conservation area. It is surely just a question of time (and probably not a long period of time) before such arguments are tested in the courts.

Even the most experienced property professionals can be caught by surprise by how far reaching and onerous the system can be (even the pre-Human Rights Act system). This book is aimed to provide a brief guide to the non-specialist practitioner and those with a general interest in the subject. It is hoped that it will highlight the main sources of potential liability and provide a means of resolving potential disputes as expeditiously as possible.

Gordon Campbell
February 2001

# · Table of Cases ·

# · Table of Statutes ·

[page references in bold indicate where the text is reproduced ]

DoE             Department of the Environment
LBPN            Listed Building Purchase Notice
LPA             Local Planning Authority
PPG2            Planning Policy Guidance Note 2 : Green Belts
PPG7            Planning Policy Guidance Note 7: The
                Countryside: Environmental Quality and
                Economic and Social Development
PPG15           Planning Policy Guidance Note 15: Planning and
                the Historic Environment
PPG16           Planning Policy Guidance Note 16: Archaeology
                and Planning
TCPA            Town and Country Planning Act 1990
TPO             Tree Preservation Order

# Dramatis Personae and Principal Functions

## Countryside Agency

- Designation of National Parks,
- The making of representations and recommendations to the Secretary of State and relevant authorities,
- Preservation and enhancement of natural beauty within the National Parks,
- Encouraging the provision and improvement of facilities.

## Secretary of State*

- Compilation and maintenance of the lists of listed buildings and the schedule of ancient monuments;
- The determination of appeals against:
  (i) the refusal and non determination of listed building consent applications,
  (ii) the issuing of listed building enforcement notices,
  (iii) refusal and non–determination of conservation area consent applications,
  (iv) the issuing of conservation area enforcement notices.
- call-in of listed building applications;
- revocation of listed building consent;
- designation of conservation areas (concurrent with Local Planning Authorities);
- issue of listed building enforcement notices (concurrent with Local Planning Authorities).

* The term "Secretary of State" is used in the relevant legislation without further statutory definition. Most of the functions referred to in the text will be exercised by the Secretary of State for Culture Media and Sport.

# · Glossary ·

| | |
|---|---|
| 1949 Act | National Parks and Access to the Countryside Act 1949 |
| 1979 Act | Ancient Monuments and Archaeological Areas Act 1979 |
| 1984 Act | Building Act 1984 |
| 1990 Act | Planning (Listed Building and Conservation Areas) Act 1990 |
| 1975 Regulations | Town and Country Planning (Tree Preservation Order) (Amendment) and Trees in Conservation Areas) (Excepted Cases) Regulations 1975 |
| 1990 Regulations | Planning (Listed Buildings & Conservation Areas) Regulations 1990 |
| 1994 Order | Ancient Monuments (Class Consents) Order 1994 |
| 1999 Regulations | Town and Country Planning (Trees) Regulations 1999 |
| AAIs | Areas of Archaeological Importance |
| AONBs | Areas of Outstanding Natural Beauty |
| BPN | Building Preservation Notice |
| Circular 36/78 | DoE Circular 36/78–Trees and Forestry |
| Circular 13/83 | DoE Circular 13/83–Purchase Notices |
| Circular 18/84 | DoE Circular 18/84–Crown Land and Crown Development |
| Circular 14/97 | DETR Circular 14/97 (also Circular 1/97 Department of Culture, Media and Sport) –Planning and the Historic Environment –Notification and Directions by the Secretary of State |
| Circular 1/2001 | DETR and DCMS Circular 1/2001 – Arrangements for Handling Heritage Applications – Notifications and Directions by the Secretary of State |
| CPO | Compulsory Purchase Order |
| DCMS | Department of Culture, Media and Sport |
| DETR | Department of the Environment, Transport and the Regions |

# Table of Statutory Instruments

# Local Planning Authorities (London Borough, Metropolitan Borough/District, District Councils)

- Determination of applications for listed building consent and conservation area consent;
- Issuing listed building enforcement notices;
- Designation of conservation areas;
- Issuing conservation area enforcement notices;
- Issuing building preservation notices;
- Revocation of listed building consent;
- Carrying out works of urgent preservation to listed buildings.

# Historic Building and Monuments Commission ("English Heritage")

- General consultation functions will regard to the exercise of the Secretary of State's powers and policies;
- Carrying out works of urgent preservation to listed buildings;
- Issue of listed building enforcement notices within London Boroughs (concurrent with Local Planning Authorities);
- Maintaining the Register of Historic Gardens.

# County Councils

- Designation of conservation areas (following consultation with the relevant District Council).

# National Park Authorities

- Sole planning authority with regard to most functions within National Parks.

# Royal Commission on the Historical Monuments of England

- Recording of important buildings at risk of demolition.

# CABE

- The Commission for Architecture and the Built Environment is an executive non-departmental public body sponsored by the DCMS. It was established on 1 September 1999 with the aim of raising architectural standards and educating both the public and the private sector as to the benefits of good architecture. It is an important consultee both at a national level and in dealing with important local projects.

# Chapter 1

# · **What is a Listed Building?** ·

## The definition

### The law

Section 1 of the 1990 Act requires the Secretary of State to compile lists of buildings of special architectural or historic interest or to approve, with or without modifications, lists compiled by the Historic Buildings and Monuments Commission (more commonly known as English Heritage). The Secretary of State may also approve lists compiled by other persons or bodies and amend any list so compiled or approved. The term "listed building" is defined as a building included in such a list.

For the purposes of the 1990 Act the following are treated as being part of the listed building:

- any objects or structures fixed to the building; and
- any objects or structures within the curtilage of such a building which, although not fixed to it, form part of the land and have done so since before 1 July 1948

(See section 1(5) of the 1990 Act.)

Furthermore, by virtue of Schedule 1 of the 1990 Act every building, which prior to 1969 was the subject of a "Building Preservation Order" under the Town and Country Planning Act 1962 is deemed to be a listed building. The Secretary of State has the power (following consultation with English Heritage) to direct that this provision does not apply to specific buildings. Upon being consulted English Heritage must in turn consult with the relevant local planning authority and the owner and occupier of the building in question.

## Confirmation of listing

Day-to-day administration of the list is carried out by the Department of Culture, Media and Sport. Unfortunately it seems that the Department has not yet had the opportunity to transfer the hard copy entries on to its website (**www.dcms.gov.uk**) a medium apparently ideal for the function. However, confirmation of whether or not a specific building is listed may be obtained by contacting the National Monuments Record (the public archive of English Heritage) at 55 Blandford Street, London W1H 3AF (phone 020 7208 8200, fax 020 7224 5333).

## Grade of listing

The most important listed buildings are categorised as "Grade I". These comprise some 9,000 buildings (approximately 2% of the total listed). The next most important are categorised "Grade II*" (another 19,000 or 4% of the total). The remainder are categorised as "Grade II". The grading of a particular building can alter as a result of re-appraisal by the Secretary of State or as a result of damage or alteration. The grading reflects the Secretary of State's opinion as to the relative merit of a building. It has no legal significance.

## The extent of listing

Contrary to popular belief (and the impression given by many entries upon the statutory list) the entirety of the building referred to on the list is listed and not just particular features which may appear to be of special interest. There are rare instances of, say, only the frontage of a building being subject to the listing procedure but such instances are very much the exception and in the absence of any express and unambiguous indication to the contrary the various protections and statutory provisions should be regarded as applying to all parts of the building referred to, and not just those parts which may be referred to in the description forming part of the statutory list.

Whilst a fixture may not be listed in isolation, the Secretary of State may take into account the desirability of preserving it when determining whether or not to list the building. Such listing will then apply to the entire building, and not just the fixture.

In determining whether or not any item is "fixed", the courts will apply the same test as in determining what is a "fixture" in other areas of property law (*Debenhams PLC* v *Westminster City Council* [1987]).

The relevant criteria to consider are the degree and purpose of annexation of the feature to the building or land. (See also *Corthorn Land and Timber Company Limited* v *Minister of Housing Local Government* [1965]; *R* v *Secretary of State for Wales ex p Kennedy* [1996]; *Berkley* v *Poulett* [1977].

The question of what should properly be considered as an "object or structure fixed to the building" was further considered in *Watts* v *Secretary of State for the Environment* [1991]. Mrs Watts purchased Bix Manor in 1977. The purchase included a small barn and various other buildings within the curtilage of the Manor. The barn was used as a garage at that time. Mrs Watts sold the Manor and a group of buildings including a larger barn in 1981. The smaller barn was retained with its own curtilage and used for storage. In 1985 the Manor House and the larger barn were listed. In accordance with the usual practice the buildings were described in brief fashion and some of the buildings originally within the curtilage of Bix Manor were not mentioned in the list. Mrs Watts carried out various works including the breach of a free-standing wall (formerly within the curtilage of the Manor) and applied for permission for change of use of the smaller barn to residential. The District Council issued a listed building enforcement notice in respect of the wall arguing that it was an "object or structure fixed to the listed building" (as per what is now a section 1(5) of the 1990 Act).

In the *Watts* case the court adopted the approach laid down by the House of Lords in the *Debenhams* case in construing the term "fixed" as meaning fixtures in the common law sense, *i.e.* as it would be construed in dealing with a property purchase or landlord and tenant matter. The court went on to consider the question of ownership and the extent to which an owner or occupier of the property would be aware that the building or structure was listed. The court held that there would be little difficulty in finding that a wall was ancillary to a listed building if at the time of the listing it served the purpose of securing the building or its curtilage and was therefore an accessory to the principal building. In the *Watts* case, at the time of listing, there was no functional relationship between the wall and the listed building. The wall was ancillary to another separate building.

In the case of *Watson-Smyth* v *Secretary of State for the Environment* [1992] the High Court adopted the same approach in upholding a listed building enforcement notice relating to a "ha-ha" (a wide ditch with a wall at the bottom providing security without spoiling the view). The ha-ha was constructed as part of the layout of the gardens of the listed

building and the functional relationship between it and the listed
building was intact at the time of listing.

## Curtilage and setting

### The law

It will be noted that listed building protection also extends to free-
standing objects or structures within the curtilage of the building which
have been *in situ* since before 1 July 1948.

Until recently the term "curtilage" was generally regarded as
meaning a small, restricted area of land used for purposes ancillary to
the building in question. See *Dyer* v *Dorset County Council* [1988] and
*Secretary of State* v *Skerrits of Nottingham Ltd* [2000] – where, at first
instance, reference was made to the "major consideration of
smallness"). The writer once attended a planning inquiry where leading
counsel traced the origin of the term back to the medieval Italian
"cortillio" – small yard or court.

Whilst the area need not be formally enclosed or maintained, the
Courts have tended to hold that areas separated or some distance from
the principal building are not within the curtilage, even within the same
ownership and occupation. Such questions have recently been revisted
by the Court of Appeal in the *Skerrits* case. Having reviewed all
relevant authorities, the court concluded "that it would be wrong to
conclude that the curtilage of a building must always be small, or that
the notion of ruralness is inherent in the expression"(per Robert Walker
LJ).

Whilst the term "curtilage" is generally regarded as having a
restricted meaning, it should be noted that local planning authorities
have special duties to take into account with regard to both:
considering listed building applications; and the general exercise of
their planning functions.

These duties extend to paying special regard to the desirability of
preserving the setting of the listed building as well as the building itself
(see sections 16 and 66 of the 1990 Act). Furthermore, special publicity
arrangements must be undertaken by a local planning authority before
it may determine any application which would, in its opinion, affect the
setting of a listed building (section 67). Clearly this extends the
geographical ambit of the LPA's considerations over a far wider area
than simply the curtilage.

## Policy

PPG15 stresses that questions of curtilage and buildings, structures and objects falling within their curtilage are ultimately questions of law for the courts to decide. However, the guidance puts forwards the following criteria to assist in determining whether or not a building apparently within the curtilage of a Listed Building is ancillary to the principal (Listed) Building and is therefore part of the listing or an independent building (*i.e.* not listed). Those criteria are:

- the historical independence of the building;
- the physical layout of the principal building and of the other buildings;
- the ownership of the buildings now and at the time of listing;
- whether the structure forms part of the land;
- the use and function of the buildings and whether a building is ancillary or subordinate to the principal building.

(See Paragraphs 3.34–3.37 of PPG15.)

That being said, it is now the practice of the Secretary of State to consider the separate individual listing of structures within the curtilage of Listed Buildings albeit that there will be cases where the listing of the principal building will extend to other buildings and structures within its curtilage.

It should be noted that the extent of the listing is not only relevant as to the application of Listed Building Control but may also have an impact upon VAT and Business Rate liability (see Chap 6).

As regards the setting of Listed Buildings, national guidance stresses:

- the setting is often an essential part of a building's character (especially where a garden or grounds have been laid out to complement its design or function);
- economic viability may suffer if buildings become isolated from their surroundings;
- LPAs should not interpret their publicity obligations too narrowly;
- setting may include land some distance from the building itself as well as land which is obviously ancillary;
- setting may encompass a number of other independent properties;
- the setting of a building may owe its character to the group value of other buildings of no particular individual merit and to the spaces between them.

The example is given of a Listed Building forming an important visual element in a street. In such circumstances it may be right to regard any development within the street as being within the setting of the building. Similarly a proposed high or bulky building may affect the setting of a Listed Building some distance away, for example in altering an historic skyline.

(See Paragraphs 2.16–2.17 of PPG15.)

# The process of listing

### The law

In considering whether or not to include a building in a list the Secretary of State may take into account not only the building itself but also:

- any respect in which its exterior contributes to the architectural or historic interest of any group of buildings of which it forms part; and
- the desirability of preserving, on architectural or historic grounds, any feature of the building consisting of any man-made object or structure fixed to it or forming part of the land comprised in the curtilage of the building.

(See section 1(3) of the 1990 Act.)

Before compiling, approving or amending any list the Secretary of State is required to consult with English Heritage and such other persons or bodies as appear appropriate as having special knowledge of or interest in buildings of architectural or historic interest (see section 1(4) of the 1990 Act).

### Policy

Buildings are included in the statutory list either as a result of the systematic survey, re-survey or review of particular areas and/or buildings or as a result of representations from concerned individuals and bodies where a building may be at risk (sometimes referred to as "spot listing"). The principal criteria which the Secretary of State will apply in determining whether or not to include a building in the statutory list are stated as being:

"architectural interest: the lists are meant to include all buildings which are of importance to the nation for the interest of their architectural design, decoration and craftsmanship; also important examples of particular building types and techniques (e.g. buildings displaying technological innovation or virtuosity) and significant plan forms;

Historic interest: this includes buildings which illustrate the important aspects of the nation's social, economic, cultural or military history;

Close historical association: with nationally important people or events;

Group value, especially where buildings comprise an important architectural or historic unity or a fine example of planning (e.g. squares, terraces, or model villages)".

The policy advice confirms, unsurprisingly, that age and rarity are other relevant considerations and continues "all buildings built before 1700 which survive in anything like their original condition are listed; and most buildings of about 1700–1840 are listed, although some selection is necessary. After about 1840, because of the greatly increased number of buildings erected and the much larger numbers that have survived, greater selection is necessary to identify the best examples of particular building types, and only buildings of definite quality and character are listed. For the same reasons, only selected buildings from the period after 1914 are normally listed. Buildings which are less than 30 years old are normally listed only if they are of outstanding quality and under threat. Buildings which are less than 10 years old are not listed." (See Paragraphs 6.10–6.12 of PPG15.)

All Local Authorities are obliged to keep copies of the lists relating to their areas available for inspection free of charge. A comprehensive record of all listings is maintained by English Heritage at its Savile Row headquarters (see Appendix 1).

# Temporary listing (building preservation notices)

### The law

Section 3 of the 1990 Act gives local planning authorities (other than County Planning Authorities) power to serve "building preservation notices". These notices may be served where the authority believes that an unlisted building in the area is of special architectural or historic interest and is in danger of demolition or alteration in such a way as to affect its character.

Whilst a building preservation notice remains in force the building in question is to be treated, for most purposes, as if it were a listed building (section 3(5)). A building preservation notice comes into force as soon as it has been served on both the owner and occupier of the building and remains in force for a maximum period of six months from the date served or, as the case may be, last served. A building preservation notice ceases to be of effect if the Secretary of State lists the building or notifies the local planning authority in writing that he does not intend to list it. If the Secretary of State gives such a notification no further notice in respect of the building may be served by the Local Planning Authority within the period of 12 months beginning with the date of the notification (see section 3(7) of the 1990 Act).

A building preservation notice may not be served on buildings which are:

- immune from listing (see "immunity from listing" – Chap 5, p40);
- in active ecclesiastical use and benefiting from the ecclesiastical exemption (see "The ecclesiastical exemption" – Chap 5, p41);
- scheduled "Ancient monument" (see Chap 9, p76);
- on Crown land (except where an interest is currently held otherwise than by or on behalf of the Crown) (see "Crown Land" – Chap 5, p46).

## Policy

National Guidance reminds authorities that the Building Preservation Notice procedure is often a quicker and more expedient short-term measure than asking the department to "spot list" a building. That being said, authorities must take into account of the possibility that they may become liable to pay compensation for loss or damage resulting from the service of a notice which is not upheld by the Secretary of State. The Secretary of State offers no guidance as to whether or not service of a notice is likely to result in a listing other than pointing out the usual general principles to be applied in deciding whether or not to list. It is pointed out that it cannot be assumed that the inclusion of a building in a draft list prepared by English Heritage will automatically result in a listing (see Paragraphs 6.23–6.25 of PPG15).

*Chapter 2*

# Consequences of Listing –
# · Enforcement Powers and ·
# Penalties

## Criminal penalties

### The law

Subject to certain specific exemptions it is a criminal offence to execute or cause the execution of any works:

- for the demolition of a listing building; or
- for its alteration or extension in any manner which would affect its character as a building of special architectural or historic interest;

unless those works are authorised (see section 7 of the 1990 Act).
The following buildings are exempt from these provisions:

- certain church buildings (see "Ecclesiastical exemption" – Chap 5 );
- scheduled "Ancient Monuments" (which benefit from their own statutory protection, – see Chap 9); and
- Crown buildings (see "Crown land" – Chap 5).

Section 9 of the 1990 Act creates two offences each triable either in the Crown Court or the magistrates' court. In addition to it being an offence to contravene section 7 outlined above (unauthorised demolition works or unauthorised alteration or extension in a manner affecting the character of a listed building as a building of special architectural or historic interest) it is also an offence to fail to comply with any conditions attached to a listed building consent. Persons guilty of such offences are liable:

- on summary conviction *i.e.* in the magistrates' court to a maximum term of imprisonment of six months and/or a maximum fine of £20,000; or
- on conviction on indictment (*i.e.* in the Crown Court) to a

maximum term of imprisonment of two years and/or an unlimited fine.

It is a defence to prove in such proceedings that:

- the works were urgently necessary in the interests of health or safety or for the preservation of the building; or
- it was not practicable to secure health or safety or the preservation of the building by works of repair or works of temporary support or shelter; or
- the works in question were the minimum measures immediately necessary;

and, in each such case that written notice giving detailed justification for the carrying out of the works was given to the LPA as soon as reasonably practicable.

In determining the amount of any fine to be imposed the court must pay particular regard to any financial benefit which has accrued or appears likely to accrue to the defendant in consequence of the offence (section 9(5) of the 1990 Act).

## Extension of penalties to certain non-listed buildings

As noted above (see Chap 1 "Temporary listing (building preservation notices)") section 3(5) of the 1990 Act operates to extend these criminal provisions to buildings which are subject to building preservation notices. Additionally, section 74(3) of the 1990 Act operates to extend these penalties to certain demolition works in conservation areas (see Chap 7).

## Proving the offence

It has been accepted by the Court of Appeal (*R* v *Sandhu* [1997]) that the offence of contravening section 7 is a strict liability offence. In the words of Bingham LCJ "the intent or state of mind or motives or knowledge of the defendant are irrelevant to the issue of guilt" albeit that such factors may be relevant in considering the appropriate penalty as opposed to the issue of innocence or guilt. The court must answer five questions:

(1) Was the building in question a listed building?

(2) If so, were the works specified in each count executed for its alteration?

(3) If so, did the defendant cause the works specified in each count to be executed?

(4) If so, were such works executed in a manner which affected the character of the building as a building of special architectural or historic interest?

(5) If so, were such works authorised?

It was further held that evidence going beyond proving these elements is inadmissible and prejudicial to the interests of the accused. By the same token an innocent state of mind cannot afford a defence.

One of the consequences of the strict nature of the liability is to render irrelevant the question of knowledge of the building's status. It is neither necessary for the prosecution to demonstrate notification nor helpful for the defendant to demonstrate lack of notification (save insofar as it may be relevant to the magnitude of any penalty).

For the prosecution to succeed it is necessary for it to demonstrate that the defendant has either executed the works in question or caused those works to be executed. This requires some positive act on the part of the defendant. It is not an offence merely to pen-nit or fail to prevent the works in question.

## Demolition or alteration?

The distinction between the terms "demolition" and "alteration" was considered by the House of Lords in the case of *Shimizu (UK) Limited* v *Westminster City Council* [1997]. It was held that whether or not the particular works in question amount to demolition or alteration is a matter of fact and degree in each case. "Demolition" was held to refer to the pulling down of the building so that it was destroyed completely or at least to a significant extent. Works involving only partial demolition (*i.e.* falling short of the entire destruction of the building) would generally be works of alteration unless they amount to a clearing of a site for redevelopment. Major works falling short of complete destruction may still constitute demolition depending upon their extent. Most works involving only part of the fabric of a building will now be regarded as "alterations".

## Authorisation of works

No offence is committed where works are authorised for the purposes of the 1990 Act. The requirements to be satisfied in determining whether or not works are properly authorised differ depending upon whether the works in question are for the alteration or extension of listed building or, alternatively, relate to demolition (in whole or in part).

In order to be authorised for the purposes of 1990 Act all such works, whether for alterations, extension or demolition, must benefit from an express listed building consent granted by the LPA or Secretary of State and must be executed in accordance with the terms and condition of that consent. However, additional requirements are imposed with regard to demolition works. In order to be "authorised" for the purpose of these provisions notice of the proposed demolition must be given to the Royal Commission (in England the Royal Commission on the Historical Monuments of England, in Wales the Royal Commission on Ancient and Historical Monuments in Wales – see Appendix 1). After such notice has been given the Royal Commission must be allowed reasonable access to the building for a period of at least one month following grant of listed building consent unless they have given written notice confirming that they have completed their recording of the building or that they do not wish to record it (see section 8(2) of the 1990 Act).

It is possible for works which would otherwise be unauthorised to be authorised retrospectively. The procedural requirements relating to applications for listed building consent and related appeals are dealt with below (see Chap 3 "Listed Building Consent Applications and Appeals").

## Authorisation by other statutory procedures

Where major development or redevelopment proposals are authorised by private Act of Parliament it is possible for provisions to be inserted in the relevant Act granting the required listed building and/or conservation area consents thereby circumventing the procedures contained in the 1990 Act. However, such provisions may now, in practice, be a thing of the past. Many major infrastructure projects which in previous times would have had to proceed by way of private Act are now subject to the relatively new procedures provided for in the Transport and Works Act 1992. In summary such projects may be authorised by means of an order made by the Secretary of State. Such orders will usually follow consideration of the proposal by means of a public inquiry. Such an order may not include provisions granting listed building or conservation area consent. However where such consent has not already been granted (*i.e.* by means of the usual procedures contained in the 1990 Act – see Chap 3) there is provision for applications being considered at the same public inquiry as that arranged to consider the proposed statutory order pursuant to the Transport and Works Act and then determined by the Secretary of State contemporaneously.

## Intentional damage to a listed building

A further offence aimed at punishing acts of vandalism (albeit limited to those acts carried out by owners and tenants) is created by section 59 of the 1990 Act. This provides that 'if a "relevant person" does or permits any act which causes or is likely to result in damage to a listed building with the intention of causing such damage he will be guilty of a summary offence (punishable by the magistrates by a fine not exceeding level 3 on the standard scale). A person is a "relevant person", for these purposes if he would otherwise be entitled to do or permit the acts in question. That is to say the offence is aimed at owners and lessees (and arguably licensees) who damage their own property. Acts of outright vandalism caused by non-owners or lessees (*e.g.* trespassers, etc) may be punished under the general criminal law (*i.e.* section 1 of the Criminal Damage Act 1971).

Section 59 provides for a degree of continuing liability for convicted defendants who fail to take reasonable steps to prevent any damage or further damage resulting from the first offence. In such circumstances the defendant will be guilty of a further offence and liable on summary conviction to a fine not exceeding one-tenth of level 3 on the standard scale for each day on which the failure continues.

A defence is provided by section 59(3) where the acts in question arise from the execution of work:

- authorised by planning permission (but only if granted pursuant to an application, *i.e.* excluding "permitted development rights" granted by statutory instrument); or
- for which listed building consent has been granted.

As is usually the case with statutory defences the burden of proof is on the defendant (to show that an appropriate permission or consent has been granted).

## Potential conflict with other statutory requirements

When dealing with dangerous buildings, the provisions of Part III of the Building Act 1984 empower local authorities to:

- apply to the magistrates' court for an Order requiring the owner to execute necessary works to obviate the danger or to demolish the building or to restrict use of the building until the court is satisfied that the necessary works have been carried out (section 77 of the 1984 Act);
- take immediate steps to remove any danger in urgent cases (section 78 of the 1984 Act);
- where the condition of the building is seriously detrimental to the amenities of the neighbourhood, serve notice upon the owner requiring the execution of repair or restoration work or, at the owner's election, demolition of the building (section 79 of the 1984 Act).

If the authority is minded to exercise its powers under either section 77 or 79 of the 1984 Act it must first consider whether or not it should exercise its powers under the 1990 Act to require the execution of works urgently necessary for the preservation of a Listed Building (section 54 of the 1990 Act, see Chap 6).

## Listed Building Enforcement Notices

In addition (or as an alternative) to instigating criminal action as outlined above, Local Planning Authorities may seek to have remedial works carried out by means of serving a "Listed Building Enforcement Notice" LBEN (see section 38 of the 1990 Act). Such Notices may be served when it appears to the LPA that works have been, or are being executed to a listed building where such works contravene section 9 of the 1990 Act (*i.e.* they are works of demolition or alteration which affect the building's character as a listed building or are being carded out in contravention of a condition attached to a Listed Building Consent). In order to serve the Notice they must consider it expedient to do so having regard to the effect of the works on the character of the building as a listed building.

## Formal requirements

An LBEN must:

- specify the alleged contravention;
- require such steps as may be specified in the Notice to be taken:
  (i) for restoring the building to its former state, or
  (ii) if the Authority consider that such restoration would not be reasonably practicable or would be undesirable, for executing such further works as may be specified in the Notice which they consider necessary to alleviate the effect of the unauthorised works; or
  (iii) for bringing the building to the state in which it would have been if the terms and conditions of any relevant Listed Building Consent had been complied with;
- specify the date on which it is to take effect (subject to an appeal being submitted – see below); and
- specify the period within which the required steps are to be taken (different periods may be specified for different steps).

Copies of LBENs must be served no later than 28 days after the date of their issue and not later than 28 days before the date specified in the Notice as the date upon which it is to take effect. Copies must be served on the owner and occupier of the listed building and on any other person having an interest in that building which, in the opinion of the Authority, is materially affected by the Notice (*e.g.* mortgagees and tenants not otherwise falling within the statutory definition of "owner"). The LPA may withdraw an LBEN without prejudice to their power to issue another or waive or relax any requirement (*e.g.* extending any period for compliance) whether or not the Notice has taken effect. Where a Notice is withdrawn or relaxed the LPA must immediately give notice to that effect to every person who has been served with a copy of the original Notice or who would be served if the Notice were re-issued.

Where it would be impracticable or undesirable to restore a listed building to its former state and the LBEN requires the execution of further work to alleviate the effect of the unauthorised works, Listed

Building Consent is deemed to be granted for those works (see section 38(7) of the 1990 Act). A specific grant of Listed Building Consent will operate to override the requirements of any prior Listed Building Enforcement Notice without prejudice to any liability arising prior to the date of the Act (see sections 44 and 8(3) of the 1990 Act).

(See Chap 7 with regard to the extension of LBENs to unlisted buildings in conservation areas.)

## Appeals against Listed Building Enforcement Notices

Section 39 of the 1990 Act grants a right of appeal against Listed Building Enforcement Notices. This right may be exercised by any person having an interest in the building (*i.e.* a proprietary interest) or by a "relevant occupier". A relevant occupier is a person who on the date the LBEN is issued occupied the building by virtue of a licence and continues so to occupy the building when the appeal is brought. An appeal may be made on any of the following grounds:

- that the building is not of special architectural or historic interest (*i.e.* that it should not have been listed in the first place);
- that the alleged contraventions have not, as a matter of fact, occurred;
- that if those alleged contraventions have occurred they do not constitute a contravention of the Act (*e.g.* where damage to a listed building has been caused accidentally or the appellant wishes to assert that the works have not affected the character of the building as a listed building);
- that the works to the building were urgently necessary in the interests of health or safety or for the preservation of the building, that it was not practicable to secure safety, health or, as the case may be, the preservation of the building by works of repair or works affording temporary support or shelter, and that the works carried out were limited to the minimum measures immediately necessary;
- that Listed Building Consent ought to be granted for the works, or that any relevant condition of such consent which has been granted ought to be discharged, or different conditions substituted;

- that copies of the Notice were not properly served;
- where the Notice requires restoration of the building that those requirements exceed what is necessary to restore it to its condition before the works were carried out;
- that the compliance period specified in the Notice is unreasonably short;
- the steps required by the Notice for the purpose of restoring the character of the building to its former state would not serve that purpose;
- where restoration is impracticable or undesirable and further works are specified to alleviate the effect of the unauthorised works that those steps exceed what is necessary alleviate that effect;
- where the Notice specifies steps to secure compliance with the terms and conditions of a Listed Building Consent that those steps exceed what is necessary to secure compliance.

Appeals must be made either by giving notice of the appeal to the Secretary of State before the date specified in the LBEN as the date upon which it is to take effect or by sending written notice to him in a properly addressed pre-paid letter which is posted at such time that, in the ordinary post, it would be delivered to him before that date (section 39(2) of the 1990 Act). Whilst the LPA should provide a standard form when serving the Notice it is not necessary to use the form in order to submit a valid appeal. A letter will suffice. Appellants must also submit a statement specifying the grounds on which the appeal is being made and such further information as may be required by the Secretary of State. This statement should be given either at the time of submitting the appeal or within 28 days of a request by the Secretary of State. If more than one ground of appeal is given and the appellant does not give the required information in respect of any ground the Secretary of State may determine the appeal without considering the grounds in question (section 39(4) and (5) of the 1990 Act). Where the appeal is made it is not possible to complain that the Notice was not duly served on the appellant (section 39(6) of the 1990 Act).

Where an appeal is brought against an LBEN the Notice shall be of no effect until the final determination or withdrawal of the appeal (section 39(3) of the 1990 Act). This provision is subject to the provisions of section 65(3A), which provide that in the event of a High Court challenge being made in relation to the appeal the Court may order that the Notice should have effect (see below – "High Court challenges relating to LBENs").

When deciding an appeal against LBEN the Secretary of State can correct any defect, error or misdescription in the Notice or vary its terms if satisfied that such amendment will not cause injustice to any party. Alternatively if he wishes to allow the appeal he may quash the Notice. If either party fails to comply with the requirements for submitting Statements within the prescribed period (see above) the Secretary of State may determine the appeal against that party and need not offer them an opportunity of being heard at a public inquiry.

In determining the appeal the Secretary of State may:

- grant Listed Building Consent for any required works;
- discharge any conditions/limitations attached to an existing Listed Building Consent and substitute alternative conditions;
- "de-list" the building in question (see section 41 of the 1990 Act and Chap 5).

## Penalties for non-compliance LBENs

### Civil/administrative

Where any steps specified in an LBEN have not been complied with within the stated period for compliance the LPA may enter the land in question and take the required steps. The LPA may then recover its reasonable expenses from the person who is the owner for the time being of the land (see section 42(1) of the 1990 Act).

Any sums paid by the owner to the LPA in respect to these provisions and any expenses incurred by the owner or occupier for the purposes of complying with LBEN are deemed to have been incurred or paid at the request of the person who carried out the works to which the notice related (see section 42(2) of the 1990 Act). LPAs have the power to sell materials removed in the execution of such works, subject to accounting for the proceeds of sale (section 276 of the Public Health Act 1936 as applied by regulation 11 of the 1990 Regulations).

Where an occupier prevents an owner from taking steps required by an LBEN he may submit a complaint to the magistrates' court who may then order the occupier to permit the necessary steps to be taken (section 289 of the Public Health Act 1936 as applied by regulation 11 of the 1990 Regulations).

Where expenses are recoverable from persons who can demonstrate that they receive the rent of the premises in question merely as agents or as trustee, their liability is limited to the total amount of money which they have had in their hands as rent (section 294 of the Public Health

Act 1936 as applied by regulation 11 of the 1990 Regulations).

As referred to below (see High Court challenges relating to LBEN's, below) there are limited opportunities to challenge the validity of a LBEN. The usual judicial review procedures are generally not available. However, an LPA's decision to enter land, carry out works and recover expenses may be open to challenge if it is considered unreasonable in the specific administrative law sense of the word (see the Court of Appeal decision in *R* v *Greenwich LBC ex p Patel* [1985]). Furthermore given the potentially onerous and financial penalties which may arise under LBENs the Courts tend to construe their terms very strictly (see the Court of Appeal in *Browning* v *Tameside Metropolitan Borough* [1997]).

### Criminal

Non-compliance with a listed building enforcement notice (see below) will also amount to a criminal offence triable either in the magistrates' court or the Crown Court. The maximum penalty in the magistrates' court will be a fine not exceeding £20,000. The fine upon conviction in a Crown Court is unlimited. In determining the level of any fine, the court is obliged to pay particular regard to any financial benefit which has accrued or appears likely to accrue to the Defendant in consequence of the offence (see section 43 of the 1990 Act).

A defendant will be acquitted if he can demonstrate:

- that he did everything he could be expected to do to secure that the steps required by the notice were taken; or
- that he was not served with a copy of the notice and was not aware of its existence. (See section 43(4) of the 1990 Act.)

## High Court challenges relating to LBENs

Section 64 of the 1990 Act provides that the validity of an LBEN shall not, except by way of an appeal under section 39 (*i.e.* an appeal against the notice to the Secretary of State – see above), be questioned in any proceedings whatsoever on any of the grounds on which such an appeal may be brought. However, it will be noted that this provision does not rule out the possibility of legal challenges on other grounds. In particular, the ability to apply for judicial review is not precluded. Furthermore, section 65 of the 1990 Act goes on the provide for possible appeals to the High Court arising from the decisions of the Secretary of State in LBEN proceedings upon a point of law. Section 65 also makes provision for the Secretary of State being required to state a case for the opinion of the High Court. However, this latter provision is subject to the requirements of rules which have yet to be made by the High Court and so the provision has not yet come into force.

Proceedings may only be brought with the leave of the High Court. An application for leave must be made within 28 days from the date on which the Secretary of State's decision was issued (*i.e.* the date on which it was posted and not the date on which it was received – (*Ringroad Investments Ltd* v *Secretary of State* (1979)). Similarly no appeal may be brought in the Court of Appeal except without the leave of the Court of Appeal or the High Court (section 65(5) of the 1990 Act). Whilst the 28-day time limit must normally be complied with a procedure exists enabling the court to extend this time limit in exceptional cases.

If the grounds of appeal are substantiated the court will remit the notice back the Secretary of State for re-hearing and re-determination by him. The court also has power to order that the enforcement notice takes effect on such terms as the court thinks fit pending the final determination of the court proceedings and any rehearing or re-determination by the Secretary of State. Such terms may include a requirement that the LPA gives an undertaking as to damages (section 36(3A) of the 1990 Act).

## Injunctions

The ability of local authorities to obtain injunctions has a tortuous legal history. Any question marks over LPA's powers in this respect evaporated with the introduction of section 44A of the 1990 Act. This provides that where an authority considers it necessary or expedient for any actual or apprehended contravention of section 9(1) or (2) of the 1990 Act (the general sanctions concerning unauthorised work) it may apply to the High Court or the county court for an injunction whether or not they have exercised or are proposing to exercise any of the other powers under the Act. The courts may grant such injunctions as they consider appropriate for the purpose of restraining a contravention. Interim injunctions are also available (subject to the usual undertaking in damages) even where the alleged lack of authorisation for works in question arises due to the LPA's own administrative errors (see *Fenland District Council* v *Rueben Rose Properties* [2000]).

# Chapter 3

# Listed Building Consent
## Applications and Appeals

## Applications – formal requirements

### The law

The 1990 Act provides that applications for listed building consent should be made to the local planning authority. Applications must be made upon the authority's standard form and must contain:

- sufficient particulars to identify the building to which it relates including a plan;
- such other plans and drawings as are necessary to describe the works which are the subject of the application; and
- such other particulars as may be required by the authority (see section 10).

The Planning (Listed Buildings and Conservation Areas) Regulations 1990 require applications to be made in triplicate.

### Policy

Annex B to PPG15 comments that, for all except the most simple projects, applications should be accompanied by measured drawings of all floor plans as well as elevational drawings of those parts of the building affected by the works proposed (external or internal). Applicants are further advised to provide two sets of drawings showing the "before and after" position with regard to the altered structure or new development. Authorities are advised not to accept applications until sufficient information has been supplied to enable a full understanding of the impact of a proposal. Further guidance (Appendix C to Circular 14/97) further advises authorities to set out in early discussions with applicants exactly what they will require.

# Ownership certificates and notification requirements

As is the case with "ordinary" planning applications an applicant need not own or occupy the building which is the subject the application. However the LPA is precluded from entertaining an application for listed building consent unless it is accompanied by a certificate confirming the ownership position, that is to say, a certificate in the prescribed form signed by or on behalf of the applicant stating that:

- at the beginning of the period of 21 days ending with the date of the application, no one other than the applicant was the owner of any part of the building to which the application relates; or
- the applicant has given the requisite notice of the application to all persons (other than themselves) who at the beginning of that period were owners of any part of the building; or
- that the applicant is unable to give a certificate in accordance with the above provisions but has taken reasonable steps (as specified) in the certificate to ascertain the relevant names and addresses, has specified those he has discovered in the certificate and has been unable to ascertain the remainder.

For these purposes the term "owner" means either the freehold owner or a lessee with the benefit of a fixed term of years of which at least seven years remains unexpired. Where notice of the application has been served on owners other than the applicant, the certificate submitted to the LPA by the applicant must set out:

- the names of the persons served;
- the addresses at which the notices were served; and
- the date of service.

(See section 11(3) of the 1990 Act.)

Save in the case of applications relating solely to the interior of Grade II listed buildings, LPAs are under an obligation to place an advertisement in local newspapers and display a site notice for not less than seven days either on or near the building. This notice must indicate the nature of the works and name a place within the locality where the application and submitted plans and documents may be inspected. The LPA must then take into account any representations received within 21 days of both the publication date and the first display of the site notice (see regulation 5 of the Planning (Listed Building and Conservation Areas) Regulations 1990).

Where a local planning authority outside London wishes to grant Listed Building Consent it must first notify the Secretary of State and give particulars of the works for which consent is required. The Secretary of State then has a 28-day period, commencing with the date of the notification, either to "call in" the application (see below) or notify the authority that he requires further time to consider possible call in. The LPA is precluded from granting Listed Building Consent within to this period unless the Secretary of State has notified them that it does not intend to call in the application. The same requirements are imposed within London with regard to applications made by English Heritage (section 13 of the 1990 Act).

As regards other applications within London similar provisions apply, save that London Borough Councils are required to give notification to English Heritage and English Heritage has the power to direct refusal and the Secretary of State retains the power to call in applications (section14 of the 1990 Act).

Section 15 of the 1990 Act gives the Secretary of State power to both:

- disapply the general notification requirements referred to above; and
- give directions requiring additional notification requirements.

The Secretary of State has exercised these powers by means of DETR/DCMS Circular 1/2001 – "Arrangements for Handling Heritage Applications – Notification and Directions by the Secretary of State".

In summary the following notification requirements must be observed by authorities dealing with Listed Building Consent applications;

- Notification to the national amenity societies (the Ancient Monument Society, the Council for British Archaeology, the Georgian Group, the Society for the Protection of Ancient Buildings and the Victorian Society) where the proposed works involve either the demolition or the partial demolition of Listed Building.
- Notification to English Heritage:
  (i)  outside Greater London for any works relating to a Grade I or Grade II* listed building or for works of demolition or substantial alteration of other (*i.e.* Grade II unstarred) listed buildings.
  (ii)  Within Greater London works to any listed building

except alterations from Grade II unstarrred buildings (excluding from this exception works to railway stations, theatres, cinemas, Thames bridges and works comprising the demolition of more than 50% of any external wall or substantial interior works to a principal, *i.e.* non-curtilage building).

Applications outside Greater London which relate to Grade II (unstarred) buildings need not be referred to the Secretary of State unless the application proposes demolition of a principal building (i.e. one listed in its own right rather than a "curtilage" building) or substantial demolition of a principal external wall or substantial part of the interior of a principal building.

Directions are also given as to notification requirements relating to applications for planning permission which affect the setting of a listed building or the character or appearance of a conservation area.

Failure by the LPA to adhere to these notification requirements may invalidate the grant of listed building consent *ab initio* – see the Court of Appeal decision in *Fenland District Council* v *Reuben Rose (Properties) Ltd* [2000]).

## "Call-in" of applications

### The law

Whilst, *prima facie*, applications for listed building consent should be determined by the local planning authority, the 1990 Act gives the Secretary for State the power to direct that applications be referred to him instead of being dealt with by the LPA (referred to on the power to "call-in" applications) (section 12). Such directions may either relate to particular applications or to applications relating to specified buildings. Applications required in consequence of major infrastructure proposals arising under section 1 or 3 of the Transport and Works Act 1992 are automatically referred to the Secretary of State. Before determining such applications, the Secretary of State must give the applicant and the LPA an opportunity of appearing before and being heard by the person appointed by the Secretary of State.

### Policy

The Secretary of State's power to call-in applications is unfettered (save for the usual common law requirement concerning rationality or "Wednesbury" reasonableness). There is little formal guidance as to when the Secretary of State is likely to call in applications. PPG15 refers to the Secretary of State being very selective and only exercising his power in a small number of cases. Cases are said to be likely to be called-in where the proposals raise issues of exceptional significance or controversy. Additionally, where the Secretary of State is considering a related planning application or compulsory purchase order, an application for listed building consent will usually be called-in unless it is clear that it may reasonably be dealt with separately (Paragraphs 3.20 and 3.21 PPG15). The courts have tended to support the view that the Secretary of State has been given a wide statutory discretion and are generally reluctant to interfere with his decisions on whether or not to call-in applications unless demonstrably unreasonable (See *R v Secretary of State ex p Newprop* [1983]; *Rhys Williams v Secretary of State* [1985]; *R v Secretary of State ex p Middlesborough Borough Council* [1988] and *Lakin Ltd v Secretary of State for Scotland* [1988]).

# Decisions and conditions

## Decisions

### The law

Subject to the above provisions relating to call-in the LPA or the Secretary of State may either grant or refuse an application for Listed Building Consent and if they grant a consent may grant it subject to conditions. In determining any application the LPA or the Secretary of State as the case may be, must have the special regard to the desirability of preserving the building or its setting or any features of special architectural or historic interest which it possesses. Where consent is granted it inures for the benefit of the building unless a condition or limitation applies to the contrary (section 16 of the 1990 Act).

Once a valid application has been received, the LPA should give notice of their decision to the applicant (or notice of the reference to the application to the Secretary of State – see above) within eight weeks of the date the application form and relevant certificate were lodged or such other period as may be agreed upon in writing between the applicant and the LPA (regulation 3(4) of the 1990 Regulations). There is no obligation to issue a decision once an appeal has been made to the Secretary of State.

Notices of the LPA's decision to approve or refuse applications and notice of any reference to the Secretary of State must be in writing. Additionally, the reasons for any refusal or for the imposition of any conditions must be stated in writing together with notice of the applicant's right to appeal (regulation 3(5) of the 1990 Regulations).

### Policy

National policy sets out for general criteria against which all applications are to be judged namely:

- the national and local importance of the building with regard to its intrinsic architectural and historic interest and rarity;
- the particular features of the building which Justified its inclusion in the list (NB the features referred to in the list description are not exhaustive);
- the setting of the building and its contribution to the local scene (see reference to "setting" above) and any substantial community benefits which would arise by virtue of the proposed work (*e.g.* economic regeneration or environmental enhancement)

(See Paragraph 3.5 of PPG15.)

The guidance also stresses the desirability of keeping historic buildings in active (usually economically viable) use. This may involve a difficult balancing exercise involving competing considerations given that the economic viability of a proposal may require alterations to the fabric of a building which may have a detrimental impact upon its special architectural or historic interest or similarly impact upon the surrounding area.

This issue, sometimes referred to as "enabling development" was considered by the Court of Appeal in *R v West Dorset District Council ex p Searle* [1998]. Planning permission was sought for residential development in the grounds of a Grade II* listed building which was in need of urgent repair. Permission was granted subject to conditions and obligations which would secure the carrying out of repairs to the listed building and the transfer of land to the LPA together with a commuted sum to secure future maintenance. Objectors challenged the legality of the LPA's action. However, the Court of Appeal concluded that, on the facts of the particular case, a proper balancing exercise had been carried out. The LPA had not acted irrationally, had not failed to take account of any material consideration and had not failed to make sufficient enquiries as to the financial necessity of the "enabling development".

Paragraph 3.9 of PPG15 refers to the aim of identifying the optimum viable use that is compatible with the fabric, interior and setting of the building. The guidance goes on to confirm that the best use will very often be the use for which the building was originally designed and a continuation or reinstatement of that use should be the first option:

- as regards alterations and extensions the national guidance refers to the following themes:
  (i) the necessity of assessing the elements that comprise the special interest of the building (these are not limited to "obvious visual features");
  (ii) the degree to which different buildings can accommodate alterations or extensions varies greatly – in some instances cumulative changes reflecting the history of the building are an aspect of the special interest whereas some examples may be sensitive to very minor alterations (*e.g.* buildings with important interiors and fittings);
  (iii) the grade of the listing is a material consideration but not in itself a reliable guide to sensitivity;
  (iv) the necessity of employing specialist expertise in assessing a proper balance of the competing considerations;
  (v) "façadism" (extensive redevelopment behind retained façades) is discouraged.

As regards proposed demolitions, the guidance stresses the policy objective of securing the preservation of historic buildings albeit that demolition may be unavoidable "very occasionally" (see Paragraph 3.16 *et seq* of PPG15). In particular demolition of any Grade I or Grade II* buildings is referred to as "wholly exceptional" requiring the strongest justification.

Prior to approving demolition of *any* listed building, the Secretary of State requires the following factors to be taken into account:

- the need for clear and convincing evidence that all reasonable steps have been taken, without success, to sustain existing uses or find viable new uses;
- that preservation in some form of charitable/community ownership is not possible;
- redevelopment would result in substantial community benefits to outweigh decisively the loss caused by demolition;
- the condition of the building and the likely cost of repairing and maintaining it taking into account its importance and the

value derived from its continued use (the Secretary of State encourages the adoption of consistent and long term assumptions);

- the adequacy of efforts made to retain the building in use;
- the merits of alternative proposals for the site.

Paragraph 3.42 of PPG15 confirms that the same criteria should be applied in assessing retrospective applications. Consent should not be granted simply because the works have already been carried out. There should be a proper assessment of whether or not consent would have been granted before the works were carried out. Whilst an application may be retrospective, any grant of consent only operates from the date it is issued. A prosecution may still arise in respect of the initial offence.

## Conditions

### The law

With the exception of consents granted authorising the retention of works already executed a condition must be imposed requiring that the authorised works must commence no later than five years from the date on which consent is granted or such other period (longer or shorter) as the authority may direct having regard to material considerations. If no such express condition is imposed the consent is deemed to be subject to a condition requiring the works to be commenced no later than the expiration of five years from the date of grant.

Other conditions may include requirements relating to:

- the preservation of particular features (either as part of the building or after severance from it);
- the making good of a damage caused to the building by the works;
- the reconstruction of the building or any part of it following execution using original materials so far as practicable and with such alterations to the interior as may be specified;
- the submission and approval of further details;
- the prohibition of demolition until the entering into of a contract for works of redevelopment and grant of planning permission for that redevelopment.

(See sections 17 and 18 of the 1990 Act.)

Section 19 of the 1990 Act enables persons interested in a listed building which benefits from a grant of Listed Building Consent to apply to the LPA for the variation or discharge of the conditions. The formal requirements referred to above with regard to the submission of applications, accompanying documentation and notification requirement apply equally to such applications. In dealing with such applications the LPA or the Secretary of State may add new conditions consequential upon any variation or discharge which is approved.

## Policy

All conditions should be necessary, relevant, enforceable, precise and reasonable in all other respects (paragraph B8 of Annex B to PPG15). The national guidance also encourages specific conditions in the following instances:

- recording buildings – in all cases of alteration or demolition LPAs should consider whether it would be appropriate to impose a condition requiring applicants to arrange a suitable programme to record features that are to be destroyed (see Paragraphs 3.22–3.24);
- later approval of details – such conditions should not be used unless authorities are satisfied that they have sufficient detail to assess the impact of the proposals. The authority should be satisfied that it has adequate information upon which to judge the application (*i.e.* as to the extent of the works, the methods to be used and the materials involved);
- restricting premature demolition – authorities should not authorise demolition unless they are certain that a new development will proceed (as mentioned above conditions can require that a contract and planning permission be in place for an authorised redevelopment scheme prior to commencement of demolition);
- as regards applications for the discharge or variation of conditions Paragraph B11 of Annex B to PPGl5 states that such applications should not be granted lightly. However "occasionally" where a condition is clearly no longer appropriate a change in the conditions may be granted without re-opening the fundamental question as to whether or not the consent should have been granted for the proposal.

# LBC appeals

Section 20 of the 1990 Act enables aggrieved applicants to appeal to the Secretary of State against:

- refusal of listed building consent;
- grant of consent subject to conditions (NB albeit that such appeals may result in a refusal of the underlying consent);
- refusal of an application for variation or discharge of conditions;
- refusal of an application for approval relating to a submission of details required by a condition (or grant of such approval subject to conditions).

As noted previously, applications should be decided within eight weeks of submission to the LPA. If no decision is forthcoming within this period the applicant may appeal to the Secretary of State against such non-determination. The LPA and the applicant may agree in writing that a longer period than eight weeks should apply. Appeals must be lodged within six months of the expiry of the eight-week period (or the longer agreed period).

Such appeals will be dealt with by inspectors appointed by the Secretary of State save where they relate to Grade I and Grade II* buildings or buildings which have benefited from grants made by English Heritage or the Secretary of State in which case they will be dealt with by the Secretary of State himself (see regulation 4(d) and (f) of the Town and Country Planning (Determination of Appeals by Appointed Persons) (Prescribed Classes) Regulations 1997).

Regulation 8 of the 1990 Regulations requires appeals to be submitted to the Secretary of State on a form obtained from him within the six-month period mentioned above. The appeal should be accompanied by copies of:

- the application;
- all relevant plans, drawings, particulars and documents submitted with the application (including a copy of the relevant ownership certificate submitted with the application);
- the notice of the LPA's decision (if any);
- all other relevant correspondence.

As with other forms of planning related appeals, only aggrieved applicants may submit and pursue the appeal. The grounds of appeal may include a claim that the building is not of special architectural or historic interest and ought to be removed from the statutory list. Similar submissions may be made with regard to buildings which are the subject of a building preservation notice (see section 21(3) and (4) of the 1990 Act).

The Secretary of State may allow or dismiss an appeal or may reverse or vary any part of the LPA's decision (whether or not the appeal specifically related to that part). He may deal with the application as if it had been made direct to him in the first instance and may exercise his power to amend the statutory list by removing from it the building to which the appeal relates (section 22(1) of the 1990 Act). Before determining the appeal, the Secretary of State must give the applicant and the LPA the opportunity of appearing before and being heard by a person appointed by the Secretary of State if either party so wishes. (section 22(2) of the 1990 Act).

## High Court challenges relating to Listed Building Consents and appeals

Sections 62 and 63 of the 1990 Act operate to restrict substantially the scope for challenging various orders and decisions. In summary a High Court challenge pursuant to section 63 is the only means by which the validity of the following may be questioned:

- an order by an LPA to restrict or modify a grant of Listed Building Consent pursuant to section 23 of the 1990 Act (whether before or after the Order has been confirmed);
- an Order by the Secretary of State revoking or modifying any Listed Building Consent pursuant to section 26 of the 1990 Act (whether before or after the Order has been confirmed);
- any decision on a called-in application pursuant to section 12 of the 1990 Act.
- any decision on an appeal pursuant to section 20 of the 1990 Act.
- any decision to confirm or not to confirm a LBPN;
- any decision to grant consent or give any direction in lieu of confirming a LBPN;
- any decision to grant listed building consent consequent on determining an appeal against a listed building enforcement notice.

The validity of such actions may only be challenged by an application to the High Court by an aggrieved person pursuant to section 63 upon the grounds that:

- the Order or decision in question is not within the powers of the Act; or
- any relevant requirements have not been complied with.

In this respect "relevant requirements" means any requirements of the 1990 Act or of the Tribunals and Inquiries Act 1992 or any secondary legislation made under those Acts which are applicable to the Order or decision in question.

Applications must be made within six weeks of the date the Order is confirmed (or in the case of revocation orders which take effect without confirmation the date on which they take effect) or, as the case may be, the date on which the action is taken (section 63(3) of the 1990 Act).

Pending final determination of the proceedings the court may make an Interim Order to suspend the operation of any Order or decision which is being questioned by the application. Upon being satisfied that the Order or decision is not within the powers of the Act or that the interests of the applicant have been "substantially prejudiced" by any failure to comply with any relevant requirements, the court may quash that Order or decision (section 63(4)).

*Chapter 4*

# Listed Building
# ˙Compensation Issues˙

## Revocation of Consent

Local Planning Authorities have the power to revoke Listed Building
Consents granted following an application albeit subject to a payment
of compensation and the rights of owners and others to make objection
to the Secretary of State.

Section 23 of the 1990 Act provides that where it appears to the LPA
that it is expedient to revoke or modify a consent granted on
application it may make an Order to that effect. In exercising this
function the LPA are required to have regard to the development plan
and to any other material considerations. The power may only be
exercised before the authorised works have been completed and any
such revocation or modification does not affect the lawfulness of any
part of the works previously carried out.

Unless the Order is formally unopposed (see below) it does not take
effect unless confirmed by the Secretary of State. Where an LPA submit
an Order to the Secretary of State for confirmation they must serve notice
upon all owners and occupiers and other persons who, in their opinion,
will be affected by the Order. The persons served must be given a period
of not less than 28 days in which they may require the opportunity of
appearing before and being heard by an inspector appointed by the
Secretary of State. The Secretary of State has the power to confirm an
Order either without modification or subject to such modifications as he
considers expedient (section 24 of the 1990 Act).

Where all owners, occupiers and other interested persons who have
been served with notice of the Order have notified the LPA in writing
that they do not object to the Order the LPA must advertise it in a local
newspaper instead of submitting the Order to the Secretary of State.
The advertisement must specify a minimum period of 28 days within
which such persons affected may notify the Secretary of State that they

wish to appear before and be heard by a person appointed for that purpose. The advertisement must also state a further minimum period of 14 days at the end of which, if no such notice is given to the Secretary of State the Order may take effect without being confirmed by him. A notice in similar form to the advertisement must be served upon all owners/occupiers and other interested person and a copy of the advertisement sent to the Secretary of State no more than three days after its publication (see section 25 of the 1990 Act).

The Secretary of State has the power to make such an Order of his own volition if he believes it expedient and paying regard to the development plan and other material considerations. The LPA must be consulted and similar notification requirements to those set out above must be complied with. Objectors have the same right to require an opportunity to appear before and be heard by an inspector. There is no requirement for any additional confirmation procedure (see section 26 of the 1990 Act). Additionally, regulation 13(8) of the 1990 Regulations gives the Secretary of State power to serve any notice which may usually be served by a local planning authority with respect to any listed building or building in a conservation area owned by LPA. There appears to be no policy guidance as to the exercise of these powers.

## Compensation for revocation

Where a person interested in a listed building has incurred expenditure in carrying out works rendered abortive by a revocation or modification Order or has otherwise sustained loss of damage directly attributable to the Order, the LPA must pay that person compensation in respect of the expenditure, loss or damage (even where the Order has been made by the Secretary of State – see sections 28 and 30 of the Act).

No compensation is payable in respect of:

- works carried out before the grant of the Listed Building Consent in question; or
- any other loss or damage (not being loss or damage consisting of depreciation in value) arising out of anything done or omitted to be done before the grant of that consent.

The expenditure incurred in the preparation of plans or upon other similar preparatory matters is taken to be included in expenditure incurred in carrying out the works.

As regards claims for the depreciation in value of the land, the rules set out in section 5 of the Compensation Act 1961 apply (*i.e.* the usual "willing seller on the open market" rules as applied in compulsory purchase cases). Interest is usually payable where compensation remains unpaid from the date of the making of the Order to the date of payment.

A claim for compensation must be in writing and served on the LPA by delivering it to the offices of the authority, addressed to the "Clerk" thereof (a somewhat archaic term in modern-day local government – presumably a letter addressed to the Chief Executive will suffice) or by sending it so addressed by prepaid post. The claim must be served within six months of the date of the decision in respect of which the claim is made or such longer period as the Secretary of State may allow in any particular case (regulation 9 of the 1990 Regulations).

## Compensation arising in relation to building preservation notices

Where a building preservation notice lapses without the building in question having been listed by the Secretary of State a claim for compensation may be submitted to the LPA by any person who has an interest in the building at the time the notice was served in respect of any loss or damage attributable to the effect of the notice (section 29 of the 1990 Act). The loss or damage will include any sums payable in respect of any breach of contract caused by having to discontinue or countermand any works to the building on account of the BPN being in force.

A claim for compensation must be in writing and served on the LPA by delivering it to the offices of the authority, addressed to the "Clerk" thereof (see above) or by sending it so addressed by prepaid post. The claim must be served within six months of the date of the decision in respect of which the claim is made or such longer period as the Secretary of State may allow in any particular case (regulation 9 of the 1990 Regulations).

### Requiring the LPA to purchase your listed building

The LBPN procedure enables owners to require the planning authority to purchase their interest in the listed building together with contiguous or adjacent land that goes with it (*i.e.* the Notice is not limited to the area which was subject to the particular application for Listed Building Consent). Several preconditions must be satisfied. The right arises where Listed Building Consent is:

- refused;
- granted subject to conditions;
- revoked; or
- modified

Additionally, the building and land in question must have become incapable of reasonably beneficial use in their existing state. Where the claim arises by reason of listed building consent being granted subject to conditions relating to the execution of works (or the consent has been modified by the imposition of such conditions) it must be asserted that the land cannot be rendered capable of reasonably beneficial use by the carrying out of the works in accordance with those conditions. Similarly it must be asserted in all cases that the land cannot be rendered capable of reasonably beneficial use by the carrying out of any other works for which listed building consent has been granted or for which the Local Planning Authority or the Secretary of State has undertaken to grant such consent (see section 32(1) and (2) of the 1990 Act).

Where a claim relates to other land as well as the building the owner who serves the Notice must be able to demonstrate that the use of the land in question is substantially inseparable from the listed building and that it ought to be treated together with the building as a single holding (section 32(3))

For these purposes the usual statutory definition of "owner" applies, *i.e.* the person, other than a mortgagee not in possession, who, whether in his own right or as trustee for any other person, is entitled to receive the rack rent of the land, or, where the land is not let at a rack rent, would be so entitled if it were so let (section 91(2) of the 1990 Act – referring to section 336 of the Town and Country Planning Act 1990).

In determining what is or what would be a "reasonably beneficial use" no account is to be taken of any prospective use which would involve:

- works requiring listed building consent other than works to which the LPA or the Secretary of State have undertaken to grant consent; or
- development consisting of:
  (i)  the rebuilding of any building in existence prior to 1 July 1948 or of any building which was in existence before that date but was destroyed or damaged after 7 January 1937,
  (ii)  the rebuilding of any building erected after 1 July 1948 which was in existence at the material date,
  (iii) maintenance, improvement or other alteration works affecting only the interior of the building and comprising the making good of war damage;

(As long as the cubic content of the original building is not exceeded.)

- the use as two or more separate dwelling houses of any building which at a material date was used as a single dwelling house.

(Section 32(4) of the 1990 Act and paragraphs 1 and 2 of Schedule 3 to the TCPA.)

LBPNs may not be based upon failure of the LPA to determine an application or on refusal of an application for approval of details. Service of an LBPN is also precluded where the LPA have served a repairs notice with a view to compulsory acquisition (see Chap 6 and section 48(5) of the 1990 Act).

## Procedure and counter-notices

An LBPN must be served within 12 months of the decision of the LPA or the Secretary of State or such longer period as the Secretary of State may allow in any particular case (regulation 12(2) of the Town and Country Planning General Regulations 1992). Policy advice set out in Circular 13/83 indicates that the Secretary of State is normally prepared to extend the time limit where the service of the Notice is delayed for good reason (*e.g.* awaiting a decision on a related Planning Appeal or negotiations with the LPA). LPAs have no power to extend the time limit.

An LPA upon whom an LBPN has been served has a period of 3 months beginning with the date of service within which to serve a counter-notice upon the owner stating either:

- that council are willing to comply with the purchase notice; or
- that another local authority or statutory undertaker specified in the counter-notice have agreed to comply; or
- hat for reasons specified in the counter-notice the council are not willing to comply and have not found any other local authority or statutory undertaker who will agree to comply with it in their place and that they have transmitted to the Secretary of State a copy of the purchase notice and the counter-notice.

(See section 33(1) and (2) of the 1990 Act.)

Where the Council or another authority or statutory undertaker agree to comply with the purchase notice they are deemed to be authorised to acquire the owner's interest compulsorily and also deemed to have served a Notice to treat on the date of service of the counter-notice (section 33(3) of the 1990 Act). Where the Council intend to serve a counter-notice stating that they are not willing to comply they must first send to the Secretary of State a copy of the proposed counter-notice and the LBPN (section 33(4)). Where the Secretary of State receives such a notification he must consider whether or not to confirm the LBPN. He must confirm the Notice where he is satisfied:

- that the building and land are incapable of reasonably beneficial use in their existing state;
- in a case where Listed Building Consent has been granted subject to conditions or modified by the imposition of conditions requiring the execution of works that the land cannot be rendered capable of reasonably beneficial use by the carrying out of those works; and
- the land cannot be rendered capable of reasonably beneficial use by the carrying out of any other works for which Listed Building Consent has been granted or for which the LPA or the Secretary of State has undertaken to grant such consent.

If the Secretary of State believes that those conditions are fulfilled in respect of only part of the land he must confirm the Notice only in respect of that part. He may not confirm the Notice unless he is satisfied that the land comprises such land contiguous or adjacent to the listed building as is, in his opinion, required:

- for preserving the building or its amenities; or
- for affording access to it; or
- for its proper control or management.

(See section 35(1) to (3) of the 1990 Act.)

If the Secretary of State believes it to be expedient to do so he may, instead of confirming the Notice:

- grant consent where the LBPN arises from a refusal of consent;
- revoke or amend conditions where the LBPN arises on account of the grant of consent subject to conditions;
- where the Notice arises on account of the revocation of consent cancel the Revocation Order; or
- where the LBPN arises due to consent being modified by an Order imposing conditions revoke or amend those conditions.

(See section 35(4).)

Where the Secretary of State believes that the land, or any part of it, could be rendered capable of reasonably beneficial use within a reasonable time by the carrying out of other works or development for which Listed Building Consent or planning permission ought to be granted he has the power to direct that if an application is made then such consent or planning permission shall be granted (section 34(5)). He may also modify the Notice by substituting another local authority or statutory undertaker for the Council upon whom the Notice was served (section 35(6)).

Before taking any of the actions listed above the Secretary of State must give notice of his proposed action to the person who served the Notice, the Council upon whom it was served and any other relevant local authority or statutory undertaker. Such Notice must specify a period (not less than 28 days from the date of service) within which any of the persons served may require the Secretary of State to give them an opportunity of appearing before and being heard by an Inspector appointed by him. (See section 34 of the 1990 Act.)

Unless the Secretary of State makes a formal decision upon the LBPN within nine months of the date of it being served or six months beginning with the date a copy of the Notice was sent to him (whichever is the sooner) the Notice is deemed to be confirmed (see section 36 of the 1990 Act).

*Chapter 5*

# Immunity, Exemptions and De-listing

## Immunity from listing

### The law

Section 6 of the 1990 Act makes provision for the Secretary of State to issue a certificate confirming that he does not intend to list a particular building. The issue of such a Certificate precludes both the Secretary of State from listing the building and the LPA from serving a building preservation notice for a period of five years beginning with the date the certificate is issued.

An application for such a certificate may be made by any person but only in circumstances where planning permission has been granted for works of alteration, extension or demolition or a planning application proposing such works has been submitted and a decision is pending.

Where an application for a Certificate of Immunity is submitted to the Secretary of State, notice of the application must also be given to the LPA and English Heritage.

### Practical points

Applications for Certificates of Immunity should be made to the Listing Branch of the Department of Culture, Media and Sport at 2–4 Cockspur Street, London SW1Y 5TH. There is no application form and no charge. Applicants should submit with their application:

- a copy of the relevant planning application or permission;
- a location plan *e.g.* Ordnance Survey map extract showing, where relevant, the position of any other listed buildings in the vicinity;
- clear up to date photographs of the main elevations;
- any information about the building;

- details of any specialised function/historical association/name of architects;
- its group value in the street scene and details of any interior features of interest.

It should be noted that a Certificate of Immunity from listing has no affect upon any conservation area designation or related control.

## Background and policy

The aim of such certificates is to provide a degree of comfort for the vendors and (more particularly) the purchasers of buildings where redevelopment may be contemplated. As confirmed in the case of *Amalgamated Investments and Property Co Ltd* v *John Walker & Sons Ltd* [1977] the risk of a building being listed is viewed by the Courts as an inherent and foreseeable risk for the purposes of a contract for sale and purchase. If a building is listed following exchange of contracts the purchaser is still obliged to proceed to complete the purchase (unless a specific contractual provision has been negotiated to the contrary). In practice, such desired comfort sought by an application for a Certificate of Immunity may prove illusory as the application itself may well result in a "spot listing" by the Secretary of State (see The Process of Listing – Chap 1). Accordingly the provisions do little to discourage summary demolition albeit that the provisions of sections 80 and 81 of the Building Act 1984 requiring prior notice of demolition to be served upon the local authority for all but the most minor of works (maximum penalty for breach being level 5 on the standard scale, currently £2,500) would still apply.

Where the Secretary of State refuses to grant a certificate, he will normally add the building to the Statutory List. When an application for a Certificate of Immunity is submitted, it is the Secretary of State's usual practice to re-assess completely the merits of the building applying his usual policy enter] a (see Chap 1). It should be noted that any recent decision by the Secretary of State not to list a building should not be taken as an indication that a Certificate of Immunity will be granted (see Paragraphs 6.28 and 6.29 of PPG15).

# The ecclesiastical exemption

Section 60 of the 1990 Act operates to provide an exception to the main listed building controls for the benefit of listed ecclesiastical buildings which are in active ecclesiastical use. Where works are being carried out and it is only those works which are preventing the building being used for ecclesiastical purposes the Act deems that the building is being so used (section 60(4) of the 1990 Act).

Buildings which are used wholly or mainly for the housing of ministers (*i.e.* rectories, vicarages, manses, etc) are excluded from the exemption (section 60(3)).

The Secretary of State has the power to make orders restricting or excluding the operation of the exemption:

- either generally or with regard to particular buildings or descriptions;
- differentiating between buildings in different areas;
- differentiating between different religious faiths or denominations;
- according to the use made of the building;
- as regards different parts of a building;
- differentiating between particular fixtures and/or curtilage structures;
- differentiating between different types of work;
- making consequential adaptations or modifications to relevant statutory provisions.

The Secretary of State may make further orders bringing individual ecclesiastical buildings back within the ambit of normal listed building and conservation area controls. Such orders are likely to be made where potentially damaging works are to be carried out without the necessary internal authorisation procedure being pursued by the church body in question.

The Secretary of State has exercised these powers through the Ecclesiastical Exemption (Listed Buildings and Conservation Areas) Order 1994 ("the 1994 Order"). The 1994 Order operates to restrict the ambit of the ecclesiastical exemption to certain types of building namely:

- church buildings;
- objects or structures within a church building;
- objects or structures fixed to the exterior of a church building; and
- objects or structures within the curtilage of a church building which, although not fixed to that building, form part of the land.

For the purposes of the 1994 Order a "church building" is defined as a building whose primary use is as a place of worship. Neither the 1990 Act nor the 1994 Order defines the terms "ecclesiastical" or "minister of religion".

There are separate, similar, provisions relating to cathedrals.

The exemption is expressed to be retained only for buildings of the following denominations:

- the Church of England;
- the Church in Wales;
- the Roman Catholic Church;
- the Methodist Church;
- the Baptist Union;
- the United Reformed Church;
- the Church of Scotland;
- the Free Church of Scotland;
- the Free Presbyterian Church.

The exemption is extended to buildings used for worship within educational establishments, hospitals, the Inns of Court and other public or charitable institutions.

The ecclesiastical exemption for listed buildings is extended to conservation area controls by virtue of section 75(1)(b) and (7) of the 1990 Act.


## Policy

The justification for the exemption arises from a commitment given by the Anglican Church that it would control works to its historic buildings through its own quasi-statutory "faculty jurisdiction" system and "pastoral measures" passed by the General Synod and approved by Parliament. As noted above the exemption has been extended to other denominations which have set up their own internal systems for controlling works which comply with a code of practice adopted by the Secretary of State. The code of practice seeks the introduction of systems within the relevant churches encompassing the following principles:

- the proposed works should be considered by a body independent of the minister; or
- congregation seeking approval;
- the independent body should have arrangements in place for:
  (i) obtaining independent expert advice;
  (ii) consulting with relevant authorities and bodies;

(iii) advertising and giving notice of the proposals;
- the independent body should take account of representations made and bear in mind the desirability of preserving historic buildings features of architectural merit and historic interest;
- there should be a clear and fair procedure for settling disputes there should be a system for dealing with any breaches of the system (including requirements for reinstatement);
- proper records should be kept; and
- appropriate arrangements should be in place to ensure proper maintenance and inspection of buildings at least every five years.

## Non-exempt church buildings

The effect of the 1994 Order is to restrict the ambit of the exemption. However, as the Order came into force on 1 October 1994 any works begun or contracted for by non-exemption denominations before 1 October 1994 continue to be exempt. For all other works the non-exempt denominations will be fully subject to the provisions of the 1990 Act.

PPG15 emphasises the importance of internal arrangements and interior furnishings the great majority of which will be deemed to be part of the listed building as "fixtures". When any proposed internal re-arrangements are proposed attention should be paid to the architectural coherence and qualities of the internal arrangements and fixtures. In particular, churches should aim to retain the spatial arrangements and fixtures relating to the principal areas of the buildings. If cleared areas are proposed for multi-purpose use consideration should be given to the possible installation of fixed seating which may be dismantled or moved. Authorities are encouraged to impose conditions to ensure that proper records are kept particularly where archaeological remains may be involved.

Where extensive internal works take place steps should be taken wherever possible and appropriate to re-use materials such as panelling either within the building or offered for similar re-use elsewhere.

When dealing with applications relating to buildings still used for worship purposes LPAs are advised to take the following issues into account in addition to the usual general policy criteria:

- are the changes needed due to a change in the congregation's worship needs do the changes arise due to changes in congregation size;

- do the changes arise with a view to accommodating other activities to help ensure the building's continued viability primarily as a place of worship;
- would the changes involve substantial structural changes such as sub-division of important existing spaces;
- would the changes involve the permanent removal or destruction of important features or their reversible re-ordering;
- would the works involve disturbing important archaeological remains.

(Paragraphs 8.10–8.12 of PPG15.)

Policy advice also encourages the re-use of redundant church buildings for social and community purposes. Conversion to other uses which would help to preserve interesting elements of the building should be pursued in preference to demolition.

## Redundant churches

Section 60(7) of the 1990 Act operates to exempt the demolition of redundant Anglican churches from Listed Building Control where the demolition works are carried out pursuant to a Pastoral Measure or a church "redundancy scheme". Section 75(2) operates to grant an equivalent exemption from conservation area control. However non-statutory procedures have been put in place with a view to ensuring that such proposals are the subject of a public inquiry where objections are lodged by the LPA, English Heritage, the Advisory Board to Redundant Churches or one of the national amenity societies (*e.g* the Ancient Monuments Society, the Council for British Archaeology, the Society for the Protection of Ancient Buildings, the Georgian Group, the Victorian Society).

It should be noted that sections 60(7) and 75(2) only benefit the Anglican Church. Other denominations must apply for listed building and conservation area consent in the usual manner should they wish to pursue total demolition of a redundant church. As mentioned above, the ecclesiastical exemption only applies to a building in current ecclesiastical use. It was held in the case of *Attorney General, exrel Bedfordshire County Council* v *Trustees of the Howard United Reformed Church, Bedford* [1976] that a building could not be "for the time being used for ecclesiastical purposes" pursuant to what is now section 60(1) of the 1990 Act when it was in the course of being demolished.

Similarly "Anglican" demolition works not covered by the Church of England's internal control system are subject to the full range of normal listed building and conservation area legislation.


# Crown land

### The law

The 1990 Act applies special rules with regard to "Crown land". This is defined as land in which there is an interest:

- belonging to Her Majesty in right of the Crown;
- belonging to a government department;
- held in trust for Her Majesty for the purposes of a government department;
- belonging to Her Majesty in right of the Duchy of Lancaster;
- belonging to the Duchy of Cornwall.

In summary, the 1990 Act provides as follows with regard to listed buildings on Crown land:

- such buildings may be listed by the Secretary of State in the usual manner;
- the principal operative provisions of the Act relating to restrictions on works, authorisation, enforcement etc. are only exercisable in respect of any interest held otherwise than by or on behalf of the Crown (*e.g.* private leasehold interests). Similarly, the compulsory purchase provisions of the 1990 Act only apply in respect of private interests;
- even where proceedings are contemplated with regard to private interests, listed building enforcement notices may only be issued and compulsory purchase proceedings commenced with the consent of the appropriate Crown authority;
- there is an absolute prohibition against the issuing of listed building enforcement notices where the works were carried out by or on behalf of the Crown to a building which was on Crown land at the time the works were carried out;
- the service of listed building purchase notices is restricted to circumstances where the owner of the private interest has offered to sell to an appropriate authority upon the usual compensation terms and that offer has been refused.

(See section 83 of the 1990 Act – extended to conservation area control by section 74(3).)

It should be noted that where the Crown is contemplating a disposal of land, the 1990 Act makes provision for the grant of both listed building consent and conservation area consent (section 84). In such circumstances, an application may be submitted by the appropriate Crown authority or any person authorised by that authority in writing. Any consent granted pursuant to such an application only benefits authorised works carried out after the land in question has ceased to be Crown land or, where the land remains in Crown ownership, to works carried out pursuant to a private interest in the land.

Such applications are submitted in the usual manner albeit that the 1990 Regulations provide that they must be accompanied by a copy of the consent granted by the appropriate Crown authority and, where appropriate, a statement confirming that there is no private interest in the land (regulations 15 and 6(1A) of the 1990 Regulations).

## Policy

Whilst Crown development is exempt from listed building control, conservation area control and indeed mainstream planning legislation, successive governments have undertaken to operate in compliance with a non-statutory system set out in the Department of the Environment's Circular 18/84 ("Crown Land and Crown Development"). These procedures involve liaison with local authorities, notification of development proposals to the usual consultees and publicity arrangements very much akin to the normal statutory procedures. Where there are unresolved objections the Crown authority in question must consider whether or not to proceed with the proposals. Where the objections are substantial they should be forwarded to the Department of the Environment, Transport and the Regions (DETR) for consideration and, if they remain unresolved, the Circular suggests the use of a procedure involving a meeting of the representatives of the LPA and the developing Crown body chaired by an Officer of DETR. A procedure based wholly upon the submission of written representations is also available.

# De-listing

As mentioned in Chapter 1, the Secretary of State has a wide discretion as to whether or not to list a building and there is no procedure for appealing against the exercise of his discretion on such matters (albeit that upon an appeal against refusal of listed building consent or issue of a listed building enforcement notice it may be asserted as a ground of appeal that the building should not have been listed in the first place). However, PPG15 confirms that the Secretary of State is prepared to review the statutory lists in the light of new evidence. Such evidence should be submitted to the listing branch the DCMS, 2–4 Cockspur Street, London SW1 together with photographs and a location plan.

The evidence must address issues of architectural and historical relevance. Where the objection is based upon the building's condition and the cost of repair or maintenance or to a proposed redevelopment it would be more appropriate to apply for listed building consent in the normal manner. Local authorities and the national amenity societies will be notified of any request to de-list.

The Secretary of State will not usually de-list if the building is the subject of an application for listed building consent or an appeal or if the LPA is contemplating action due to unauthorised works or neglect.

In 1986 the Department of the Environment issued informal guidance to the effect that, for an application to be successful, the Secretary of State had to be persuaded that either:

- a mistake had occurred in putting the building on the list; or
- that the building had become so altered or mutilated that it was no longer worthy of protection.

Once an application is received, it is forwarded to English Heritage who appoint an expert to examine the site. Applicants can request that they accompany English Heritage's representatives upon a site visit.

# Chapter 6

# Positive Planning for the Historic Environment

## Urgent preservation works

Where it appears to a local authority that works are urgently necessary in respect of a listed building within their area, they have the power (subject to certain limitations) to carry out those works. As regards listed buildings in England, the Secretary of State has the power to authorise English Heritage to carry out such works. In Wales he may execute such works himself.

The works in question only extend to works of temporary support or shelter for the building. The owner of the building must be given at least 7 days, written notice of the authority's intention to carry out the works. It has been held that the notice should if specify the necessary works in detail (see *R v Secretary of State for the Environment ex p Hampshire County Council* [1981] and *R v London Borough of Camden ex p Comyn Ching and Co (London) Ltd* [1983]). The Act requires that the notice must describe the proposed works (see section 54 of the 1990 Act).

Within Greater London English Heritage may exercise such functions concurrently with the relevant London Borough Council.

Where the building in question is occupied, such works can only be carried out to those parts of the building which are not in use.

Where authorities are minded to exercise their "dangerous building" powers under the Building Act 1984, they must first consider whether or not they should take action under those provisions or sections 47 and 48 of the 1990 Act (compulsory acquisition/repairs notices – see below).

Where an authority has incurred expenses executing such works, section 55 of the 1990 Act enables that authority to serve notice on the owner of the building requiring him to reimburse those expenses. Where the works consist of or include works for affording temporary support or shelter, the expenses which may be recovered include any continuing expenses in respect of apparatus or materials used. Additional notice re-claiming expenses incurred may be served from time to time in respect of ongoing expenses.

An owner served with such a notice has a period of 28 days in which to make representations to the Secretary of State to the effect that:

- some or all of the works are unnecessary for the preservation of the building; or
- in the case of temporary work, that the arrangements in question have continued for an unreasonable amount of time; or
- the amount specified in the notice is unreasonable; or
- recovery of the expenses would cause hardship.

(See section 55 of the 1990 Act.)

It has been held that the submission of a bill alone to the land owner by an authority is not a proper giving of "notice" for the purposes of these provisions. Similarly an advance warning is not seen as sufficient. Written notice cases should be given indicating that the council wish to exercise a statutory power to seek reimbursement – *Bolton Metropolitan Borough Council* v *Jolley* [1989].

A local authority is entitled to recoup reasonable sums in respect of their overheads or "establishment charges" (section 36 of the Local Government Act 1974).

# Acquisition of historic buildings

Powers to acquire buildings of special architectural or historic interest voluntarily are vested in local planning authorities (county, county borough, district and London borough) by section 52 of the 1990 Act. There is no requirement that the building in question be listed, in a state of disrepair or even within the relevant council area. The power extends to any land comprising of contiguous or adjacent to the building in question which appears to the Secretary of State to be required for:

- preserving the building or its amenities;
- affording access to it; or
- its proper control or management.

Where it appears to the Secretary of State that reasonable steps are not being taken for the proper preservation of a listed building, he may authorise the LPA for the area in which the building is situated to acquire it compulsorily or acquire it compulsorily himself (see section 47 of the 1990 Act).

The Secretary of State may not make or confirm such a Compulsory Purchase Order (CPO) unless he is satisfied that it is expedient to make provision for preservation of a building and to authorise its compulsory acquisition for this purpose. Where the building is situated in England he must also consult with English Heritage.

The usual procedural rules prescribed by the Acquisition of Land Act 1981 apply to such compulsory acquisitions with the following modifications:

- within 28 days of service of notice of the order a lessee or occupier (except the tenant for a month or less) may apply to the magistrates' courts for an order staying further proceedings on the CPO on the basis that reasonable steps have been taken for proper preservation of the building (see section 47(4), (5) and (6) of the 1990 Act);
- CPO proceedings under section 47 may not be started unless at least two months previously the owner of the building has been served with a "repairs notice" (see section 48 of the 1990 Act).

A repairs notice must specify the works which the appropriate authority or, as the case may be, the Secretary of State considers reasonably necessary for the preservation of the building. The notice must also explain the effect of the following provisions of the 1990 Act:

- section 47 (the possibility of compulsory acquisition);
- section 49 (general assumptions as to compensation); and
- section 50 (the power of the appropriate authority to direct "minimum compensation" (*i.e.* compensation being restricted to the market value of the building as it stands with no account being taken of possible development value). Where the authority are satisfied that the building has been deliberately allowed to fall into disrepair for the purpose of justifying its demolition and the development or redevelopment of the site by any adjoining site.

The House of Lords *Robbins* v *Secretary of State for the Environment* [1989] drew a clear distinction between works of "preservation" as opposed to "restoration" albeit that the works required by a repairs notice could include works necessary to secure "preservation" as at the date of the listing of the building. The scope of the notice was not limited by the state of the building at the time the notice was served.

Upon completion of a compulsory acquisition under these provisions all private rights of way are extinguished together with rights of laying down erecting, continuing or maintaining any apparatus on under or over the land (save for all rights vested in or apparatus belonging to statutory undertakers or telecommunications code system operators) (see section 51 of the 1990 Act).

### Policy

PPG15 confirms that it is the Secretary of State's view that, wherever possible, privately owned historic buildings should remain in the private sector. All authorities are encouraged to identify the private individuals or bodies with access to funds to whom any buildings which are acquired compulsorily may be sold on subject to covenants ensuring that repairs are carried out (see Paragraph 7.13 of PPG15).

## Management of acquired properties

Where a local planning authority acquire property either compulsorily or voluntarily it may make such arrangements as to management of the property, its use or disposal as it considers appropriate for the purpose of its preservation (see section 53(1) of the 1990 Act). The same provision applies to property acquired voluntarily by English Heritage.

Where the Secretary of State acquires property compulsorily he may:

- make such arrangements as he thinks fit as to its management, custody or use; and
- dispose or otherwise deal with any such building or land as he may from time to time determine.

English Heritage may be party to such arrangements with the Secretary of State (see section 53(2) and (3)). The Court of Appeal in *Rolf* v *North Shropshire District Council* [1988] held that it was lawful for the local authorities to compulsorily purchase property pursuant to section 47 with a view to its immediate disposal to another body.

## Grants

Section 57 of the 1990 Act enables local authorities to contribute towards the expenses incurred or to be incurred in the repair or maintenance of both listed buildings within or within the vicinity of their areas and also other buildings within the area which, although not listed, appear to the authority to be of architectural or historic interest. At the time of making such a contribution the authority may also contribute towards the expenses incurred, or to be incurred, in the upkeep of any garden occupied with the building and contiguous or adjacent to it.

Contributions may be made by grant or loan and where made by loan such loan may be interest-free if the authority so determines. Authorities may also renounce the right to repayment of any loan or interest which remains outstanding or agree to vary any other terms and conditions upon which the loan was made. Authorities can require as a condition of any grant that the person to whom the grant was made shall enter into a agreement allowing public access to the property.

If during the period of three years beginning with the date the grant was made the grantee disposes of his interest in the property by way of sale or exchange or by way of lease for a term of at least 21 years the authority may recover the amount of the grant, or such part of it as it thinks fit, from the grantee (section 58). If the grantee donates the whole of his interest in the property to any person otherwise than by will the repayment provisions take effect as if the donee were the original grantee (see section 58(2) and (3)). Additionally authorities have the power to recover grants where a condition imposed is contravened (section 58(4)). It should be noted that the conditions attached to such a grant are not local land charges and the liability to repay is personal to the grantee or donee as the context so requires.

Sections 4 and 4A of the Historic Buildings and Ancient Monument Act 1953 gives similar power to the Secretary of State to make and recover grants for the preservation of historic buildings, their contents and adjoining land.

Section 77 of the 1990 Act gives English Heritage the power to make grants or loans for the purpose of defraying expenditure which in its opinion will make a significant contribution towards the preservation or enhancement of the character or appearance of any conservation area situated in England or any part of such area. The Secretary of State has a similar power in respect of conservation areas in Wales. Section 78 imposes similar repayment provisions to those contained in section 58 referred to above. English Heritage may also enter into "town scheme agreements" with one or more local authorities to the effect that a specified sum of money will be set aside for a specified period for the purposes of making grants for the repair of identified buildings (see sections 79 and 80 of 1980 Act).

## Exemption from "empty" business rates

Historic buildings are exempt from the usual requirement to pay business rates upon unoccupied premises. The Non-Domestic Rating (Unoccupied Property) Regulations 1989 operate to grant an exemption for unoccupied business properties where the relevant rating "hereditament" is:

- the subject of a building preservation notice;
- is a listed building;
- is a scheduled monument.

Where a building is only listed in part it appears that the exemption will not apply unless the part which is not listed can be described as an object or structure affixed the listed building and lies within its curtilage (see *Providence Properties Ltd* v *Liverpool City Council* [1980] and *Debenhams Plc* v *Westminster City Council* [1987]; *Richardson Developments Ltd* v *Birmingham City Council* [1999].

## Zero-rating for VAT purposes

By virtue of section 30 and Schedule 8 (Group 6) of the Value Added Tax Act 1994 the supply of various goods and services is "zero-rated" for the purposes of calculating VAT. The supply of:

- any services (other than those of an architect, surveyor or any person acting as consultant or in a supervisory capacity); and
- building materials

will be zero rated where they relate to an "approved alteration" of a listed building or scheduled monument which is:

- designed to remain as or become a dwelling or number of dwellings;
- intended for use solely for a relevant residential purpose; or
- intended for a relevant charitable purpose.

"Approved alteration" means:

- any alteration to a building benefiting from the ecclesiastical exemption (see Chap 5); and
- any works which require listed building consent or, as the case may be, scheduled monument consent (or would require such consent if not for the existence of a Crown interest) and for which consent has been granted.

Works of repair or maintenance and incidental works are specifically excluded.

# Chapter 7

# · Conservation Areas ·

## Designation

### The Law

All local planning authorities are under an obligation to determine, from time to time, which parts of their area are of special architectural or historic interest the character or appearance of which it is desirable to preserve and enhance and then designate those areas as "conservation areas". There is a further duty to review the past exercise of this function and determine whether a further area should be designated (section 69(2) of the 1990 Act). The Secretary of State also has power to designate conservation areas (see section 69 (3)). Prior to exercising his powers the Secretary of State must consult with the relevant local planning authority. Should a County Planning Authority wish to make a designation it is obliged to first consult with the relevant District Council. Within London such designation may also be made by English Heritage subject to prior consultation with the relevant London borough and obtaining the consent of the Secretary of State.

A local planning authority making a designation or varying or cancelling an earlier designation must notify the Secretary of State and, if it affects an area in England, English Heritage. Similarly if the Secretary of State makes a designation he must if notify the relevant local planning authority and English Heritage. Notice of any designation, variation or cancellation must be given in the *London Gazette* and at least one local newspaper circulating in the relevant area (see section 70).

It has been held that a conservation area designation can extend to areas upon which there are no buildings (*R v Canterbury City Council, ex p Halford* [1992]).

### Policy

PPG15 advises authorities that are considering whether or not to designate a conservation area that:

"It is the quality and interest of areas rather than that of individual buildings which should be the prime consideration in identifying conservation areas."

It is suggested that the following factors be taken into account:

- the historic layout of property boundaries and thoroughfares;
- the "mix" of uses;
- characteristic materials;
- appropriate scaling and detailing of contemporary buildings;
- the quality of advertisements, shop fronts, street furniture and hard and soft surfaces;
- the vistas along streets and between buildings; and
- the extent to which traffic intrudes and limits pedestrian use of space between buildings.

In reviewing designations authorities are urged to bear in mind that the concept of designation should not be devalued by the designation of areas lacking any special interest. Consistent local standards should be established and existing conservation areas reviewed against those standards. Cancellation should be considered where there is no longer any special interest in an area. The principle concern should be to form a judgement on whether the area is of special architectural or historic interest the character or appearance of which it is desirable to preserve or enhance. It is suggested that authorities may take into account the resources likely to be required both for administering conservation area controls and also consulting with local residents and formulating policies for the area.

Whilst there is no statutory requirement to engage in any consultation exercise prior to designation the guidance urges that it is highly desirable that there should be consultation with local residents businesses and other interest groups over both the identification of the areas and the definition of their boundaries. Whilst, in law, a simple resolution of the authority would suffice to effect a designation in practice most authorities pursue conservation area designation and associated policies through the development plan (*i.e.* the Local Plan or UDP procedures pursuant to Part II of the TCPA) process and the extensive consultation arrangements which that entails.

# General duties

## The law

Local planning authorities are under a duty to formulate and publish proposals for the preservation and enhancement of their conservation areas. Such proposals must be submitted for consideration to a public meeting and the authority must have regard to any views expressed by persons attending the meeting (section 71 of the 1990 Act).

More importantly, from the point of view of day to day practice in exercising any of their functions under the planning acts (and certain related grant making powers) with regard to any building or other land within a conservation area, authorities must pay special attention to the desirability of preserving or enhancing the character or appearance of that area (see section 72 of the 1990 Act).

For many years it was argued, and indeed held by the courts, that this requirement obliged applicants to demonstrate some form of positive benefit arising from proposed development. The concept of avoiding harm was essentially negative and not sufficient to discharge the burden imposed by section 72 (*Steinberg* v *Secretary of State for the Environment* [1989]). This approach was overruled by the House of Lords in the case of *South Lakeland District Council* v *Secretary of State for the Environment* [1992] when it was ruled that the requirement to preserve the character or appearance of a conservation area can be achieved by development which would not have an adverse effect. There is no obligation to positively enhance.

Where a development proposed by a planning application would, in the LPA's opinion, affect the character or appearance of the conservation area they are under an obligation to publish a statutory notice in a local newspaper and post a site notice for a minimum period of seven days. Notification must also be sent to English Heritage and the application may not be determined before the expiry of 21 days beginning with first publication of the notice in the local press or, if later, the date on which the site notice was first displayed (see sections 73 and 67 of the 1990 Act).

## Policy

Paragraph 4.14 of PPG15 emphasises the Secretary of State's opinion that the desirability of preserving or enhancing conservation areas is a material consideration in an LPA's handling of development proposals even those which are outside the conservation area but which would affect its setting or views in to or out of the area. The publicity requirements imposed by section 73 are designed to draw attention to this requirement. The guidance also stresses the importance of having relevant policies contained in the authority local plan together with a clear indication of the relationship between the plan and detailed assessments or statements relating to particular conservation areas.

However, particularly when dealing with commercial areas, authorities are instructed to avoid unnecessarily detailed controls over businesses and households whilst ensuring that new development accords with the area's special architectural and historic interest. The development of "gap" sites or buildings which may detract from the character of the area should be seen as an opportunity to enhance the area not necessarily by imitation of earlier styles. Design briefs are encouraged.

# Control of demolition

## The law

Perhaps the principal consequence of conservation designation is the imposition of extensive demolition controls. Subject to certain exceptions, buildings within conservation areas may not be demolished without "conservation area consent" granted by the local planning authority (or granted by the Secretary of State where it is the LPA who wishes to demolish).

The question of what works amount to "demolition" was considered by the House of Lords in the case of *Shimizu (UK) Ltd* v *Westminster City Council* [1997]. It as held that "demolition" refers to the pulling down of a building so that it is destroyed completely or at least to a very significant extent. However, works which involve demolition of only part of a building, falling short of its entire destruction, would generally be regarded as works of alteration unless they amount a clearing of the site for redevelopment. Major works falling short of complete destruction may still constitute demolition depending upon their extent. Accordingly most works involving only part of the fabric of a building will now be regarded as alterations and will not be the subject of conservation area control (albeit that they would require listed building consent if the building was in fact listed and the works affected the character of that building as a listed building. Perhaps unhelpfully from the practitioner's point of view, their Lordships held that whether or not works amounted to "demolition" or "alteration" was a question of fact and degree to be determined on the merits of each case.

Unauthorised demolition of an unlisted building in a conservation area is a criminal offence and the various punitive and administrative provisions of the listed building regime are applied to conservation area controls with necessary modifications (see section 74(3) of the 1990 Act). Accordingly:

- similar penalties may be imposed and statutory defences claimed (see Chap 2);
- applications may be made for "conservation area consents", appeals may be pursued and such consents may be the subject of revocation procedures as is the case with listed building consents (see Chap 3);
- conservation area enforcement notices may be issued and be the subject of appeals to the Secretary of State;
- purchase notices may be served by owners;
- dangerous structure orders may be made; and
- orders decisions and notices may be the subject of High Court challenges (see sections 2 and 3).

## Policy

PPG15 offers very little in the way of policy direction when dealing with conservation area consent applications. Authorities are reminded of the requirement to pay special attention to the desirability of preserving or enhancing the character or appearance of the area. Authorities are also instructed to take account of the part played by the building in question in the architectural or historic interest of the area and in particular the possible wider effects which demolition would have upon the building's surroundings and the conservation area as a whole.

There is a general presumption in favour of retaining buildings which make a positive contribution to the area. Proposals to buildings in conservation areas should be assessed against the same broad criteria as proposals to demolish listed buildings (see Chap 3). In less clear-cut cases the LPA should obtain full information about what development is proposed for the site after demolition. Consent should not be granted unless there are acceptable and detailed plans for the intended redevelopment and the merits of the proposed redevelopment are a material consideration in determining whether or not consent should be granted for demolition. Indeed conditions may be imposed prohibiting the commencement of demolition work until such time as a contract has been entered into for the carrying out of an acceptable redevelopment scheme as is the case with listed building applications (see section 17(3) of the 1990 Act as applied to conservation areas by section 74(3)).

### Consultation paper arising from the Shimizu judgment

On 19 January 2000 DETR and DCMS issued a joint consultation paper on whether the legislation required further amendment as a result of the *Shimizu* decision. In summary the government do not propose to make any change to the current listed building consent regime. Partial demolition still requires a specific grant of listed building consent where the works are likely to affect the special architectural or historic interest of the building. However, it was considered that a new requirement may be justifiable in requiring applications for planning permission to be submitted for certain works to unlisted building within a conservation area, namely:

- the demolition of all or part of a boundary wall, gate, fence or other means of enclosure;
- the removal, without replacement, of chimney stacks on dwelling houses;
- the removal, without replacement, of porches on dwelling houses.

At the time of publication the results of this consultation exercise are still awaited.

# Exclusions from demolition control

The provisions controlling demolitions in conservation areas do not apply to:

- listed buildings (which are the subject of their own controls (see Chaps 1, 2 and 3));
- scheduled monuments (again, subject to their own control regime (see Chap 9));
- ecclesiastical buildings in active ecclesiastical use and subject to the ecclesiastical exemption (see Chap 5);
- buildings which are the subject of a Direction made by the Secretary of State pursuant to section 75(2) of the 1990 Act – see below.

**The Secretary of State's Direction**

Section 75(2) of the 1990 Act gives the Secretary of State powers to direct that conservation area controls do not apply to certain descriptions of buildings. Circular 1/2001 sets out the direction (Paragraph 31) confirming that the usual demolition controls in conservation areas do not apply to the following:

(a) any building with a total cubic content not exceeding 115 cubic metres (external measurement) or any part of such a building, other than a pre-1925 tombstone;

(b) any gate, wall, fence or other means of enclosure which is less than one metre high where abutting on a highway (including footpaths and bridleways), waterway or open space, or less than two metres high in other cases;

(c) any building erected since January 1914 and in use, or last used, for the purposes of agriculture or forestry;

(d) any building required to be demolished by virtue of an order made under section 102 of the TCPA (orders requiring discontinuance of use or alteration or removal of buildings or work).

(e) any building required to be demolished by virtue of any provision in an agreement made under section 106 of the TCPA 1990;

(f) any building whose demolition is required, in whole or in part, by the provisions of an enforcement notice issued pursuant to section 172 of the TCPA or a listed building enforcement notice issued pursuant to section 38 or 46 of the 1990 Act;

(g) any building required to be demolished by virtue of a condition contained in a planning permission granted pursuant to an application or appeal;

(h) any building whose demolition is required by an order served under section 215 of the TCPA (orders requiring proper maintenance of land);

(i) any building which is the subject of a demolition order or a confirmed compulsory purchase order made under the "unfitness" provisions of the Housing Act 1985;

(j) a redundant ecclesiastical building pursuant to the Pastoral measure 1983.

# Trees in conservation areas

Trees within conservation areas benefit from protection akin to that applying to trees which are the subject of a Tree Preservation Order (TPO) (see Chap 8). Section 211 of the TCPA provides that, subject to certain exceptions, any person who cuts down, tops, lops, uproots, wilfully damages or wilfully destroys a tree in a conservation area shall be guilty of an offence triable either in magistrates' court (maximum fine £20,000) or the Crown Court (unlimited maximum fine). In determining the level of any fine to be imposed the court must have regard to the financial benefit which has accrued or appears likely to accrue to the defendant in consequence of the offence.

It is a defence for a person charged with breaching this requirement to prove:

- that the defendant served notice of his intention (with sufficient particulars to identify the tree) on the LPA in whose the tree is or was situated; and
- that he did the act in question:
  (i) with the consent of the LPA or
  (ii) after the expiry of six weeks from the date of the notice but before the expiry of the period of two years from that date.

(See section 211(3) of the TCPA).

The purpose of this notification requirement and the period of delay prior to the execution of the works is to give the LPA an opportunity to consider making a specific tree preservation order.

## Exempted cases

Section 212 of the TCPA 1990 gives the Secretary of State power to make regulations disapplying the general prohibition against unauthorised work to trees in conservation areas. This power has been exercised by means of the Town & Country Planning (Trees) Regulations 1999 (and prior to 2 August 1999 by means of the Town & Country Planning (Tree Preservation Order) (Amendment) and (Trees in Conservation Areas) (Exempted Cases) Regulations 1975). These regulations provide that section 211 of the TCPA (the general prohibition against felling, lopping, topping, etc above.) shall not apply in the following circumstances:

- the cutting down, uprooting, topping or lopping of a tree which is dead, dying or dangerous or where works are carried out to comply with a statutory obligation or when necessary for the prevention or abatement of a nuisance or in the circumstances set out in Article 5 of the prescribed form of TPO (see Appendix 2);

- the cutting down of a tree in accordance with a felling licence granted by the Forestry Commissioners or in compliance with positive covenants imposed on a landowner in a forestry dedication deed or in accordance with a plan of operations approved by the Forestry Commission under such a deed;
- the cutting down of a tree which is in accordance with a plan of operations approved by the Forestry Commission under an approved woodland scheme or under the conditions of a grant or loan pursuant to the Forestry Act 1967;
- the cutting down, uprooting, topping or lopping of a tree by or on behalf of a local planning authority;
- the cutting down, uprooting, topping or lopping of a tree having a diameter not exceeding 75 millimetres, or the cutting down or uprooting of a tree having a diameter not exceeding 100 millimetres where the act is carried out to improve the growth of other trees (a reference to "diameter" being construed as a reference to the diameter measured over the bark at a point 1.5 metres above ground level).

### Policy

When considering whether or not to extend protection to trees in conservation areas LPA's should always take into account the visual historic and amenity contribution of trees (Paragraph 4.40 of PPG15).

The LPA must maintain a register of such notices containing the following particulars:

- the address of the land on which the tree stands and sufficient information to identify the tree;
- details of the work proposed;
- the date of the notice and who served it;
- the decision (when made) of the LPA in respect of the tree, the date of the decision and the name of the authority; and
- an index for tracing entries.

(See section 214 and Schedule 1 paragraph 14 of the TCPA and Circular 36/78)

## Additional tree enforcement controls

In addition to the criminal penalties referred to above, the local planning authority have power to require the replacement of trees which are removed, uprooted or destroyed in breach of the general conservation area controls imposed by section 211 of the TCPA as set out above. Section 213 of the TCPA provides that it is the duty of the land owner in such circumstances to plant another tree of an appropriate size and species at the same place as soon as he reasonably can, unless he makes application to the LPA who grant a dispensation. The duty to replace the tree in question, attaches to any owner of the land from time to time. Should the owner fail to comply voluntarily, the LPA has a four year period in which it may serve notice upon the owner requiring him within such period as may be specified, to plant a tree or trees of such size and specifies as may be stated in the notice. The period for compliance should not be less than 28 days beginning with the date of service of the notice (see sections 213, 206 and 207 of the TCPA).

The person upon whom such a notice is served, may appeal to the Secretary of State against the notice on any of the following grounds:

- that the relevant statutory provisions are not applicable in the instant case or have been complied with;
- that in all the circumstances of the case the duty to plant a replacement should be dispensed with;
- that the requirements of the notice are unreasonable in respect of the period for compliance as stated in the notice or the size or species of trees specified;
- the planting of a replacement or replacements in accordance with the notice is not required in the interests of amenity or would be contrary to good forestry practice;
- that the place at which the tree is or trees are required to be planted is unsuitable for that purpose

The notice of appeal should indicate the grounds of appeal and state the facts on which it is based. The appeal should be submitted to the Secretary of State before the expiry of the period for compliance specified in the notice.

On any such appeal, the Secretary of State must provide an opportunity for the parties to be heard if either of them so desires. Where an appeal is submitted, the notice is of no effect until the final determination of withdrawal of the appeal. The Secretary of State has power to correct any effects, errors or mis-descriptions in the notice and may vary any of its requirements if he is satisfied that the correction or variation will not cause injustice to the appellant or the LPA. On determination of such an appeal, the Secretary of State may quash the notice and give directions as necessary to give effect to his determination.

# Chapter 8

# · Landscape ·

## The Countryside Agency

The Countryside Agency (formerly called the Countryside Commission) is given the following functions by section 1 of the National Parks and Access to the Countryside Act 1949:

- the preservation and enhancement of the natural beauty in England within the areas designated as both National Parks or as areas of outstanding natural beauty;
- encouraging the provision or improvement of facilities for the enjoyment of those areas including open-air recreation and the study of nature.

Similar functions are vested in the Countryside Council for Wales by virtue of section 130(2) of the Environmental Protection Act 1990.

The Secretary of State has power to issue direction "of a general character" as to the manner in which the agency or the Council exercise their functions (see section 3 of the 1949 Act).

## National Parks – general

The Countryside Agency has the power to make orders designating National Parks where it considers it desirable for the purpose of conserving and enhancing the natural beauty, wildlife and cultural heritage of the area in question. Such areas must be "extensive tracts of country" which appear by reason of their natural beauty and the opportunities therefore to open air recreation to be such as to make it especially desirable that they be designated as a National Park (section 5 of the 1949 Act).

The Agency has general duties to make recommendations and representations to the Secretary of State and relevant authorities with regard to the functions of the National Parks in addition to the following specific duties:

- to give advice to appropriate planning authorities;
- to assist authorities in formulating proposals for securing the provision of accommodation and access for open-air recreation and other facilities for visitors;
- to give advice when consulted by the Secretary of State in connection with planning matters;
- to make recommendations to the Secretary of State and other ministers where it considers development proposals to be inconsistent with the maintenance of the area as a National Park;
- to notify the Secretary of State or other ministers of action which needs to be taken in considering future development proposals; and
- where they are not satisfied that their recommendations or advice on any of the above matters will not be given effect, to refer the matter to the Secretary of State and advising us that the exercise make powers of direction or enforcement under the 1949 Act or the TCPA.

(See section 6 of the 1949 Act.)

## Designation and variation of the National Parks – procedure

The Countryside Agency must consult with every Joint planning board, county council and district council before making an order designating a National Park in respect of land within their administrative area. Such an order must describe the relevant area by reference to a map and such other description as the commission considers requisite (see section 7 of the 1949 Act). The First Schedule to the 1949 Act, sets out advertisement and other administrative arrangements to be followed in making a designation order. The Secretary of State can vary an order designating a National Park subject to prior consultation with the Countryside Agency and any National Park authority, joint planning board, county council and district council affected by the proposed variation. The advertisement and administrative arrangements set out in the First Schedule similarly apply to such variations.

The following National Parks are currently designated:

- Brecon Beacons;
- Dartmoor;

- Exmoor;
- Lake District;
- North York Moors;
- Northumberland;
- Peak District;
- Pembrokeshire Coast;
- Snowdonia;
- Yorkshire Dales.

At the time of going to press proposals are in hand for the designation of the South Downs and the New Forest as National Parks (England's first since the 1950's). The Broads have not been designated as a National Park but similar considerations and administrative arrangements apply pursuant to the Norfolk and Suffolk Broads Act 1988 (see section 5 of the TCPA).

## Planning functions

Within the English National Parks located outside the metropolitan counties, most planning functions are vested in the county planning authority. Certain functions are exercisable concurrently by county and district planning authorities, namely:

- making provisional Tree Preservation Orders (sections 201 of the TCPA);
- serving and enforcing tree replacement notices (sections 206–209 of the TCPA);
- tree preservation controls in conservation areas (sections 211–214 of the TCPA);
- injunctive powers relating to the above (sections 214A–214D of the TCPA);
- service of land maintenance notices (section 215 of the TCPA).

Section 2 of the TCPA gives the Secretary of State power to constitute joint planning boards for National Parks. However, these provisions have been superseded by the National Park Authority created under the Environment Act 1995. Section 4A of the TCPA provides that where a new National Park Authority has been established (under section 65 of the Environment Act 1995), that authority is the sole planning authority for the park save for the tree and land maintenance related provisions which may also be exercised by the District Council concurrently.

In preparing development plans or alterations or additions thereto for an area including the whole or any part of the National Park, the authority preparing the plan, must consult with the countryside agency and take into account any observations made.

The general duty imposed by section 11 of the Countryside Act 1968 should always be taken into account, namely:

> "in the exercise of their functions relating to land under any enactment, every minister, government department and public body shall have regard to the desirability of conserving the natural beauty and amenity of the countryside".

Both the Secretary of State and local planning authorities have compulsory purchase powers in respect of "any open country" which they consider the public should have access to for open air recreation (sections 76 and 77 of the 1949 Act). The following may not be the subject of compulsory purchase pursuant to these provisions:

(1) agricultural land (save for rough grazing);
(2) formally declared nature reserves;
(3) land covered by buildings or the curtilages of such land;
(4) paths, gardens or pleasure grounds in active use;
(5) land used for surface mineral working, railways, tramways, golf courses, racecourses or aerodromes;
(6) land used by statutory undertakers (or telecommunications operators);
(7) land in the course of development which will result in it coming within paragraphs 3, 5 or 6 above;
(8) land to which section 193 of the Law of Property Act 1925 applies (commons and "manorial wastes").

(See section 60 of the 1949 Act.)

Section 14 of the 1949 Act gives the Secretary of State power to acquire by agreement, any land in the National Park by way of purchase, lease or exchange subject to the consent of the Treasury. Any land so acquired must be transferred to other persons on trust or subject to such conditions as appear to the Secretary of State to be expedient to secure the simple management of the land (unless the Secretary of State considers otherwise).

## Policy

General policy guidance on planning issues in the countryside is contained in Planning Policy Guidance Note 7 (PPG7: The

Countryside: Environmental Quality and Economic and Social Development). With specific regard to the National Parks, the Guidance confirms that such designation confers the highest status of protection with regard to landscape and scenic beauty.

The Guidance goes on to provide that the conservation of the natural beauty of the countryside and its wildlife and cultural heritage should be given priority and weight both in terms of determining planning policy and exercising more day to day development control decisions. Consideration must also be taken of economic and social issues with regard to local communities, however major development should not take place within National Parks, the Broads or the New Forest Heritage Area save in exceptional circumstances. Major developments should only proceed if demonstrably in the public interest. In considering such applications, the following issues should be considered:

- the need for the development in terms of national considerations, and the impact of permitting it or refusing it upon the local economy;
- the cost of and scope for developing elsewhere outside the area or meeting the need for it in some other ways;
- any detrimental affect on the environment and the landscape, and the extent to which it should be moderated.

(Paragraph 4.5 of PPG7.)

Within the New Forest Heritage Area the same planning principles apply as apply to the National Parks albeit that all development plan and development control matters will be dealt with by the appropriate local planning authorities.

Given the likely impact upon issues such as public enjoyment and other environmental considerations, it is likely that major applications will require submission of an environmental statement pursuant to the Town and Country Planning (Environmental Impact Assessment) (England and Wales) Regulations 1999. Further guidance on the need for and the contents of such a statement is given in DETR Circular 2/99.

## Areas of Outstanding Natural Beauty

### The law

Section 87 of the 1949 Act gives the Countryside Agency power to designate areas of outstanding natural beauty (AONBs) and sets out the administrative arrangements to be followed in implementing such a designation. Such designations cannot include land within the area of a National Park and it is generally accepted that the designation should cover a smaller geographical area than the National Parks. There are no special statutory arrangements for administering AONBs or policies relating thereto.

Landscape protection within AONBs is exercised through the normal planning policy and development control functions of local planning authorities.

## Policy

PPG7 requires that in general planning policies and development control decision should favour conservation of the natural beauty of the landscape and that the environmental affect to the proposals will be a major consideration, though authorities must have regard to economic and social issues also. It is generally regarded as inconsistent with the aims of designation to permit major industrial or commercial development within AONBs. Only proven national interest and lack of alternatives sites, should justify exceptions being that (Paragraph 4.8 of PPG7). Applications for new or extended mineral workings must be subject to rigorous appraisal as must new road schemes.

## Secretary of State's statement on AONBs

In April 1991 the then Secretary of State issued a statement touching upon the general principles relating to planning within and the management of AONBs. He confirmed that the conservation and enhancement of natural beauty should continue to be the primary objectives of AONB policy and that recreation is not an appropriate objective for designation. However, he recognised the role played by AONBs in meeting demand for recreation which should continue so far as that role is consistent with AONB purposes.

The Secretary of State confirmed that AONB designation conferred formal recognition and that the natural beauty of the area is of national importance and worthy of protection. He expected this to be reflected by local authorities in their preparation of development plans and in the exercise of development control functions. The provision of "Statements of Intent" to clarify the role and purpose of designating new AONBs and the provision of management plans was encouraged. These should be taken into account in the planning process, particularly where AONBs crossed county and district boundaries where a consistent approach was desirable. However, it was recognised that many mineral deposits occurred within the more beautiful parts of the countryside including national parks and AONBs and essential sources of supply could not be dispensed with.

## Green Belt

Whilst the primary objective of Green Belt designation is one of development control rather than landscape protection, national guidance (PPG2 – Green Belts and PPG7 see above) stress that the openness of Green Belts is their most important attribute. Strictly speaking Green Belt designation is a policy matter and has no statutory force. However national guidance stresses the great weight given to Green Belt designation in planning policy terms. This is reflected in local policy making and development control decisions and is further supported by section 54A of the TCPA which requires that:

> "Where, in making any determination under the planning acts, regard is to be had to the development plan, the determination shall be made in accordance with the plan unless material considerations indicate otherwise".

PPG2 provides that the five purposes of green belts are:

(1) to protect the unrestricted sprawl of large built-up areas;
(2) to prevent neighbouring towns from merging into one another;
(3) to assist in safe-guarding the countryside from encroachment;
(4) to preserve the setting and special character of historic towns; and
(5) to assist in urban regeneration by encouraging the recycling of derelict and other urban land.

The objectives of the Green Belt designation are expressed to be:

- to provide opportunities for access to the open countryside for the urban population;
- to provide opportunities for outdoor sport and outdoor recreation near urban areas;
- to retain attractive landscapes and enhance landscapes near to where people live;

- to improve damaged and derelict land around towns;
- to secure nature conservation in trust, and to retain land in agricultural, forestry and related uses.

The policy guidance provides for a strong presumption against "inappropriate development". The construction of new buildings inside the Green Belt is deemed inappropriate unless for the following purposes:

- agriculture and forestry;
- essential facilities for outdoor sport and outdoor recreation, for cemeteries, and for other uses which preserve the openness of the Green Belt, and do not conflict with its purposes;
- limited extension, alteration or replacement of existing dwellings;
- limited infilling in existing villages and limited affordable housing for local community needs pursuant to development plan policies;
- limited infilling or redevelopment of major existing developed sites identified in adopted local plans.

These national policies tend to be reflected in county structure plans, local plans and UDPs and adhered to with greater rigour and consistency than most development plan policies.

# Historic gardens

Section 8C of the Historic Buildings and Ancient Monuments Act 1953 requires English Heritage to compile a register of gardens in England which appear to them to be of special historic interest. As soon as is practicable after making an entry in the register, English Heritage are obliged to notify the owners and occupiers of the garden or land in question, the relevant planning authorities and the Secretary of State.

Inclusion of the garden within the register, gives rise to no special protection, save for drawing the importance of the land in question, to the attention of the relevant authorities. PPG15 advised local planning authorities to protect registered parks and gardens through the development plan system and in determining planning applications. The effect of a proposal on a registered park and garden, or in setting is stated to be a material consideration in determining planning applications. Planning authorities are also advised to safeguard registered parks and gardens when planning new developments or road schemes (see Paragraph 2.24 of PPG15).

In September 1994 English Heritage published a draft "Battlefields Register" intended in due course to be comparable with the parks and gardens register. The intention of the proposed register is to identify a limited number of areas of historic significance where important battles are sufficiently documented to be located on the ground. Once complete, the contents of the register will need to be taken into account by local planning authorities as a material planning consideration.

## Tree preservation orders

Where it appears to a local planning authority that it is expedient in the interests of amenity to make provision for the preservations of trees or woodlands in their area they may make an order with respect to:

- individual trees;
- groups of trees; or
- woodlands.

Such orders (Tree Preservation Orders) may, in particular, make provision for:

- prohibiting (subject to specified exceptions) the felling, topping, lopping, uprooting, wilful damage or wilful destruction of protected trees except with the consent of the LPA (which concern may be conditional);
- securing replanting; and,
- procedural matters relating to applications for consent to fell or carry out other works to protected trees.

(See section 198 of the TCPA 1990.)

A model form of order is set out in the Schedule to the Town & Country (Trees) Regulations 1999 (see Appendix 2 for the model form of order). The model order sets out various exemptions from TPO control for statutory undertakers and other utilities. Works in commercial orchards are exempt but the exemption relating to work on other fruit trees only extends to pruning in accordance with good horticultural practice. A guide to good practice was published by the DETR on 17 April 2000 (see **www.wildlife.countryside.detr.gov.uk/ tpo/guide**).

Breach of the provisions of a TPO is a criminal offence punishable by a maximum fine of £20,000 in the magistrates' court or an unlimited fine in the Crown Court. In determining the level of any fine the court

# Chapter 9

# · Archaeology ·

## Ancient monuments – designation

### The law

The Secretary of State is under a statutory duty to compile and maintain a schedule of monuments (section 1 of the Ancient Monuments and Archaeological Areas Act 1979 "the 1979 Act").

When the Schedule was first prepared upon the introduction of the 1979 Act the Secretary of State was obliged to include within it all monuments protected under previous legislation. Thereafter he has had a discretion to include further monuments which appear to him to be of national importance. Before exercising this discretion the Secretary of State must consult with English Heritage. The Secretary of State has further powers to exclude monuments from the schedule (again, subject to prior consultation with English Heritage) and also to amend existing entries. The Secretary of State is precluded from including within the schedule any structure occupied as a dwelling other than accommodation occupied by caretakers.

The term "monument" may include:

(1) any building, structure or work, whether above or below the surface of the land, and any cave or excavation;
(2) any site comprising the remains of such building, structure or work or of any cave or excavation; and
(3) any site comprising, or comprising the remains of, any vehicle, vessel, aircraft or other moveable structure or part thereof which neither constitutes nor forms part of any work which is a monument within the paragraphs above

Any machinery attached to a monument shall be regarded as part of the monument if it could not be detached without being dismantled (section 61(7) of the 1979 Act).

The definition is extended to include not only the land in or upon which the monument itself is situated but also adjoining land which appears to the Secretary of State, English Heritage or the local authority when exercising their respective functions to be essential for the monument's support and preservation (section 61(9) of the 1979 Act).

Certain buildings and structures are excluded:

- ecclesiastical buildings in current ecclesiastical use are excluded from the ambit of paragraph (1) above;
- sites comprising objects or their remains are excluded from the ambit of paragraph (3) unless they are so sited as to be a matter of public interest;
- sites protected pursuant to the Protection of Wrecks Act 1973 are also excluded from paragraph (3).

The term "monument" is also deemed to include the site of the monument in question and, in appropriate cases, a group of monuments or any part of an individual monument or group of monuments (section 61(7)–(10) of the 1979 Act).

The term "ancient monument" means a monument included within the statutory schedule by the Secretary of State or any other monument which is in his opinion of public interest by reason of the historic, architectural, traditional, artistic or archaeological interest attached to it (section 61(12) of the 1979 Act).

The Secretary of State is under an obligation to keep English Heritage informed of all decisions he makes with regard to the schedule. As soon as they have been informed of the Secretary of State's decisions, English Heritage must inform the owner and occupier of the monument and any local authority in whose area the monument is situated and also publish the relevant information (section 1A of the 1979 Act).

## Control of works

It is a criminal offence to execute or cause or permit the execution of the following works without written authorisation from the Secretary of State:

- works resulting in the demolition or destruction of a scheduled monument;
- works resulting in any damage to a scheduled monument;
- any works removing or repairing a scheduled monument or any part of it;
- making any alteration or addition to a scheduled monument;
- flooding or tipping operations on land in, on or under which there is a scheduled monument.

Such offences are triable either in the magistrates' court or the Crown Court. On summary conviction the maximum fine may not exceed the statutory maximum (currently £5,000). Upon conviction in the Crown Court there is no limit upon the level of fine (section 2 of the 1979 Act).

In any proceedings it is a defence to prove that the works were urgently necessary in the interests of health or safety and that written notice of the need for the works was given to the Secretary of State as soon as reasonably practicable. Where the offence relates to works resulting in demolition or destruction of or damage to a scheduled monument the accused will have a defence if he can prove that he took all reasonable precautions and exercised all due diligence to avoid or prevent damage. Similarly where the offence relates to demolition, destruction, damage or flooding or tipping operations, the accused will have a defence if he can prove that he did not know and had no reason to believe that the monument was within the area affected by the works or, as the case may, that it was a scheduled monument. Where the offence relates to the breach of any condition attached to a consent the accused will have a defence if he can prove that he took all reasonable precautions and exercised all due diligence to avoid the contravention in question.

Works are authorised for the purposes of the Act if:

- the Secretary of State has granted written consent ("scheduled monument consent") for the execution of the works; and
- works are executed in accordance with the terms of the consent and of any conditions attached to it.

Consent may be granted either unconditionally or subject to conditions. Such conditions can govern the manner in which the works are to be executed or the person by whom they should be executed. Conditions may be attached requiring that a person authorised by English Heritage be given an opportunity to carry out an examination of the monument and its site (including works of excavation) for the purposes of archaeological investigation prior to the commencement of any of the works.

Unless specified to the contrary within the consent it will lapse following the expiry of five years from the date on which it was granted unless the authorised works are executed or started (section 4 of the 1974 Act).

The Secretary of State has power to make orders, following consultation with English Heritage, granting scheduled monument consent for specified classes or descriptions of works. The Secretary of State has further power to issue directions excluding the effect of such an order from specific monuments. Again he is under an obligation to consult with English Heritage prior to making or withdrawing any such directions.

If such a direction is issued thereby requiring a specific application for scheduled monument consent to be submitted a liability to compensation may arise if such application is refused or granted subject to conditions (see section 9 of the 1979 Act – below).

The Secretary of State has exercised his powers and granted a wide ranging list of consents by means of the Ancient Monuments (Class Consents) Order 1994. This grants general consent for the following classes of works subject to stated limitations, namely:

## Agricultural, horticultural and forestry works

Such works are permitted provided that they are of the same kind as works previously carried out lawfully in the same location and on the same spot within that location within the period of six years immediately preceding the commencement of the work. The following are excluded:

- in the case of ploughed land, works likely to cause disturbance below the depth at which the ploughing has previously been carried out lawfully;
- on non-ploughed land, any works likely to cause disturbance below a depth of 300 millimetres;
- sub-soiling, drainage works, the planting or uprooting of trees, hedges or shrubs, the stripping of topsoil, tipping or the commercial putting or removal of turf;
- demolition, removal, extension, alteration or disturbance of any building, structure or work or remains;
- the erection of any building or structure;
- the laying of paths, hard standings or foundations for buildings or the erection of fences (other than in the case of domestic gardening works).

## Coal mining operations

Works carried out more than 10 metres below ground level are permitted when carried out by an operator licensed under the Coal Industry Act 1994 or the Coal Industry Nationalisation Act 1946.

## Works by the British Waterways Board

Works carried out by the Board are permitted in relation to land owned or occupied by them being works of repair or maintenance not involving a material alteration to a scheduled monument where those works are essential for the purpose of ensuring the functioning of a canal.

## Repair or maintenance of machinery

Works for the repair or maintenance of machinery are permitted where they do not involve a material alteration to a scheduled monument.

## Urgent health or safety works

Works are permitted if they are urgently necessary in the interests of safety or health provided that:

- the works are limited to the minimum immediately necessary; and
- written notice giving detailed justification of the need for the work is submitted to the Secretary of State as soon as reasonably practicable.

## Works by English Heritage

Any works executed by English Heritage are permitted.

## Archaeological evaluation

Works of archaeological evaluation are permitted if carried out by or on behalf of a person who has applied for consent under the 1979 Act and provided that the works are carried out:

- in order to supply the Secretary of State with information he requires in order to determine that application;
- under the supervision of a person approved in writing by the Secretary of State and in accordance with a written specification approved by him.

## Pursuant to certain statutory agreements

Section 17 of the 1979 Act (see "Acquisition, Guardianship and Management of Monuments" below) provides for agreements being entered into between the Secretary of State or English Heritage and the occupiers of monuments to enable works of maintenance or preservation to be carried out. The 1994 Order authorises such works as are executed in accordance with the terms of such an agreement.

### Certain grant aided work

Section 24 of the 1979 Act gives English Heritage extensive powers to defray or contribute towards the cost of various projects. The 1994 Order operates to grant consent for work for preserving maintaining or managing a scheduled monument where the works are executed in accordance with a written agreement governing such defrayal or contribution.

### Works by the Royal Commission on the Historical Monuments of England

The Royal Commission may place survey markers to a maximum depth of 300 millimetres for the purpose of measured surveying of visible remains.

## Other criminal sanctions

In addition to the general provisions concerning the execution of unauthorised works, section 28 of the 1979 Act provides that it is an offence to destroy or damage any protected monument without lawful excuse knowing that it is a protected monument and either intending to destroy or damage the monument or being reckless as to whether or not it would be destroyed or damaged. Works done by or with the permission of the monument's owner with the benefit of scheduled monument consent are excluded from the ambit of this offence. The term "protected monument" extends not just to scheduled monuments but also to monuments under the ownership or "guardianship" of English Heritage or a local authority by virtue of the 1979 Act (see below).

Offences are triable either in the magistrates' court or the Crown Court. Upon conviction in the magistrates' court the maximum penalty is a fine not exceeding the statutory maximum (currently £5,000) or a term of imprisonment not exceeding six months or both. On conviction on indictment in the Crown Court, the maximum fine is unlimited and the maximum term of imprisonment is 2 years. Furthermore, where the owner or any other person is convicted of an offence involving damage to a monument which was at the time of the offence under the guardianship of English Heritage or a local authority the courts may make a Compensation Order in favour of English Heritage or the local authority (section 29 of the 1979 Act and section 35 of the Powers of the Criminal Courts Act 1973).

Section 42 of the 1979 Act restricts the use of metal detectors within the sites of scheduled monuments or any monuments under the ownership or guardianship of English Heritage or a local authority. Any person using a metal detector in such a place without the written consent of English Heritage is guilty of an offence and punishable in the magistrates' court to a fine not exceeding £200. Furthermore a person removing any object of archaeological or historical interest which he has discovered by the use of a metal detector in such a place is liable to a fine in the magistrates' court not exceeding the statutory maximum (currently £5,000).

## Acquisition, guardianship and management of monuments

The 1979 Act gives the Secretary of State power to compulsorily purchase ancient monuments for the purpose of securing their preservation together with any adjoining land or land in the vicinity which appears to the Secretary of State to be reasonably required for:

- maintenance of the monument or its amenities;
- providing or facilitating access to the monument;
- the exercise of proper control or management with respect to the monument;
- the storage of equipment or materials needed for maintenance purposes; or
- the provision of facilities and services to the public for or in connection with public access.

(See sections 10 and 15 of the 1979 Act.)

The usual CPO procedures set out in the Acquisition of Land Act 1981 are applicable. However, for valuation purposes it is assumed that scheduled monument consent would not be granted for any works which might result in the demolition, destruction or removal of the monument or any part of it (section 10(4)). Before exercising his powers of compulsory purchase the Secretary of State is under an obligation to consult with English Heritage.

Powers to acquire voluntarily and accept gifts of ancient monuments are vested in:

- the Secretary of State (following consultation with English Heritage);
- English Heritage (with the consent of the Secretary of State); and
- any local authority as regards monuments situated in or in the vicinity of their area.

(See section 11 of the 1979 Act.)

Any land acquired by the Secretary of State, English Heritage or a local authority under these provisions may be disposed of albeit that local authorities and English Heritage must first consult with the Secretary of State and the Secretary of State must consult with English Heritage before exercising these powers. Such disposals may only take place on such terms as will, in the opinion of the relevant body, ensure the preservation of the monument unless they are satisfied that it is no longer practicable to preserve it (on reasons of cost or otherwise) (see section 30 of the 1979 Act).

The 1979 Act also contains provisions governing the concept of "guardianship" (sections 12–15). These provisions enable a person who holds a specified legal interest in an ancient monument to enter into a deed either with the Secretary of State or the local authority vesting full control and management of the monument in the Secretary of State or the local authority as the case may be. Such deeds may be entered into by:

- freeholders;
- lessees with a term of years of which not less than 45 years remains unexpired or renewable for a term of not less than 45 years;
- persons with life interests under an existing or future trust for sale under which the estate or interest subject to the trust is either freehold or leasehold with 45 years unexpired or renewable for not less than 45 years; and
- limited companies and most forms of trustee with such an interest.

A person who is not the occupier of the monument cannot establish such guardianship arrangements unless the occupier is also a party to the deed. No such arrangements may be entered into in respect of structures which are occupied as dwellinghouses by persons other than caretakers of the monument.

Before entering into such arrangements the Secretary of State must consult with English Heritage. English Heritage itself may become guardian with the consent of the Secretary of State.

The provisions of such guardianship deeds are binding upon successors in title and, accordingly, should be registered as local land charges (section 12(7) of the 1979 Act).

Subject to any provision to the contrary in the guardianship deed, the guardian has powers or do all such things as may be necessary for the maintenance of the monument and may in particular:

- make any examination;
- open up the monument or make excavations for the purposes of examination; and
- remove the whole or any part of the monument to another place for the purpose of preserving it.

The term "maintenance" is defined as including fencing, repairing and covering in of the monument and any other act or thing required for the purpose of repairing or protecting the monument from decay or injury.

Guardianship may be terminated by an occupier who has sufficient interest in the monument to establish guardianship arrangements but who is not bound by the deed in question. Alternatively the guardian (*i.e.* Secretary of State, English Heritage or local authority) may agree with persons who are bound by the guardianship deed either to exclude part of the monument from the guardianship or to renounce guardianship.

Section 19 of the 1979 Act confirms that the public shall have access to any monument under the ownership or guardianship of the Secretary of State, English Heritage or a local authority subject to their powers to make regulations governing such access and prescribing charges.

Section 17 of the 1979 Act enables less formal arrangements to be entered into either by the Secretary of State or English Heritage with the occupiers of ancient monuments with respect to:

- maintenance and preservation;
- the carrying out of work;
- public access;
- restrictions upon use; and
- financial contributions from the Secretary of State or English Heritage.

# Compensation arrangements for scheduled monuments

Section 7 of the 1979 Act sets out the limited circumstances in which compensation is payable for refusal of scheduled monument consent. Where a person with an interest in the whole or any part of the monument incurs expenditure or sustains loss or damage in consequence of a refusal, or the granting of a scheduled monument consent subject to conditions, English Heritage are under an obligation to pay that person compensation in respect of that consequential loss or damage provided that the works in question fall within any of the following heads:

- works reasonably necessary for carrying out any development for which planning permission has been granted (otherwise than by a General Development Order made by the Secretary of State, *i.e.* pursuant to a planning application) before the monument became scheduled and which was still valid as at the date the application was made;
- works which do not constitute development for the purposes of the TCPA;
- works which constitute development but for which planning permission is granted by a General Development Order; and
- works which are reasonably necessary for the continuation of any use of the monument for a purpose for which it was used immediately prior to the date the application for scheduled monument consent was made (excluding any use in contravention of any legal restriction applying to the use of the monument).

The compensation payable in respect of any works relating to planning permission granted prior to scheduling are limited to expenditure incurred or other loss or damage sustained by virtue of the fact that due to the Secretary of State's decision any development could not be carried out without contravening the general prohibition against carrying out works without scheduled monument consent.

There is no entitlement in respect of works which do not constitute development or constitute development for which permission is granted by a general development order if the works in question, or any other works, would or might result in the total or partial demolition or destruction of the monument unless the works consist solely of operations involved in or incidental to the use of the site for the purposes of agriculture or forestry.

Where scheduled monument consent is granted subject to conditions, no entitlement to compensation arises in respect of work reasonably necessary for the continuation of any use of the monument taking place prior to the relevant application unless compliance with the conditions would make it impossible to use the monument for that use.

In calculating the depreciation in value of an interest in land it is to be assumed that:

- any subsequent application for scheduled monument consent for works of a like nature would be determined in the same way; but
- if, in the case of a refusal of scheduled monument consent, the Secretary of State undertook to grant consent for some other works regard shall be had to that undertaking.

The right to compensation extends to circumstances where works cease to be authorised by virtue of consent being varied, revoked or modified (see section 9 of the 1979 Act).

Where compensation has been paid and consent is subsequently granted or conditions modified in respect of work for which compensation was paid, section 8 of the 1979 Act provides for recovery of that compensation by the Secretary of State, or English Heritage as the case may be.

The quantum of compensation relating to depreciation in the value of land is calculated by reference to the same rules as set out in the Land Compensation Act 1961 for the purpose of compulsory purchase (with necessary modifications). That is to say, the objective is to compensate on the basis of the impact upon the market value of the land. Where land is subject to a mortgage the compensation payable should be assessed as if the relevant interest in the land were not subject to the mortgage. Compensation may be claimed by any mortgagee (without prejudice to the ability of any other person to make a claim). Any compensation payable shall be first paid to the mortgagee (or the first mortgagee where there is more than one) as if it were the proceeds of sale (see section 27 of the 1979 Act).

# Archaeological areas – designation

Part II of the 1979 Act provides for the designation by the Secretary of State, English Heritage or Local Authorities of Areas of Archaeological Importance (AAIs). The purpose of the system is to introduce a compulsory period of delay to projects which may disturb important remains thereby enabling appropriate investigations to be carried out and records compiled. This system may be regarded as a back-up to the powers of planning authorities to impose conditions in planning permissions requiring the carrying out of investigations (see below) or, at least, access to be provided to appropriately qualified investigatory authorities. The provisions of the 1979 Act apply regardless of whether or not planning permission is required or specific planning conditions have been applied.

Section 33 of the 1979 Act enables the Secretary of State, to make orders designating AAIs as regards any areas which appear to him to merit such treatment subject to prior consultation with English Heritage. English Heritage may also make such orders as regards any area within Greater London. Local authorities are similarly empowered to make such orders, subject to prior notification of English Heritage, albeit that local authority designation orders must be confirmed by the Secretary of State. The Secretary of State has power to vary or revoke any designation order (again, subject to prior consultation with English Heritage) but may only vary an Order by reducing the area to which it applies.

Proposals to make a designation order must be published in two successive weeks in the *London Gazette* and in at least one local newspaper circulating in the relevant locality. Copies of the draft order and map must be deposited with each local authority whose area is affected by the designation prior to first publication of the proposal.

The Secretary of State may proceed to make the order (modified or otherwise) following the expiry of six weeks from the date of first publication. The making of the order must also be publicised for two successive weeks in the *London Gazette* and a local newspaper. The order only comes into effect following the expiry of six months following the date on which it was made. Similarly a designation order made by a local authority or English Heritage and confirmed by the Secretary of State does not come into operation until the expiry of six months beginning with the date of confirmation (see Schedule 2 of the 1979 Act).

## Effect of AAI designation

It is a criminal offence to carry out or cause or permit to carrying out of operations within an AAI:

- without first serving an "Operations Notice" (see below); or
- within six weeks of serving such a Notice.

These provisions relate to:

- any operations which disturb the ground;
- flooding operations; and
- tipping operations

subject to certain exemptions (see below). Offences may be tried either in the magistrates' court or the Crown Court. The maximum penalty in the magistrates' court is a fine not exceeding the statutory maximum (currently £5,000). The maximum penalty in a Crown Court is an unlimited fine (see section 35 of the 1979 Act).

## Exempt operations

The Areas of Archaeological Importance (Notification of Operations) (Exemption) Order 1984 provides that the notification requirements do not apply to the following:

- operations connected with agricultural, horticultural or forestry use provided that they do not disturb the ground lower depth than 600 millimetres;
- operations connected with landscaping (including screening by the erection of fences or walls), layout, planting, or maintenance of public or private gardens, grounds or parks provided that they do not disturb the ground below a depth of 600 millimetres;
- tunnelling or other operations affecting the ground at a depth of 10 metres or more;
- mining operations carried out in accordance with the code of practice for mineral operators;
- repair, renewal or maintenance or emergency works carried out by a drainage body or navigation authority;
- repair, maintenance relaying or re-surfacing of a highway or footpath as defined in the Highways Act 1980 or of a railway provided that such operations do not disturb the ground below a depth of 600 millimetres or the existing foundations whichever is deeper;
- repair, maintenance or renewal of mains pipes cables or other apparatus connected with the supply of electricity, gas, water,

drainage, services, sewerage services, highway or transport authority services or telecommunication service;

- the installation or laying of new mains, pipes, cables or other apparatus etc where there is a statutory duty to undertake those operations and to do so within 6 months of the duty first arising;
- the erection or re-positioning of street lighting columns not involving excavations in excess of 1.5 metres in depth.

## Notification procedures

A person carrying out or proposing to carry out the operations ("the developer") is required to serve an operations notice in the prescribed form accompanied by a certificate in the prescribed form (see Appendix 2).

The Notice should specify:

- the operations in question;
- the site on which they are to be carried out;
- the date on which it is proposed to commence; and
- where the operations are to be carried out after site clearance, the date which the developer estimates as being the likely date for completion of the clearance.

The accompanying certificate must state whether the developer:

- has an interest in the site of the operations entitling him to carry out the operations in question;
- has a right to enter into possession of the site pursuant to compulsory purchase powers; or
- is a statutory undertaker entitled to carry out the operations pursuant to a specified statutory provision.

The operations notice and certificate must be served upon:

- in England – the District Council or London Borough Council (or each one in whose area the operations are wholly or partly situated);
- in Wales – the County Council;
- where the developer is a Council – the Secretary of State.

(See section 35 of the 1979 Act.)

On receipt of an operations notice, the Council should serve a copy of it (together with a copy of the accompanying certificate and any other relevant documents received) upon the relevant "Investigating Authority" (see below) or, where there is no such authority, upon English Heritage (when the site is in England) or the Secretary of State (with regard to sites in Wales).

Where the operations described in the Notice are to be carried out following clearance of the site, the Council must give written notice to the developer within 14 days of receipt of the operations notice of the name and address of the relevant investigating authority and inform the developer of his duty to notify the investigating authority immediately on completion of the clearance operations (see the Operations in Areas of Archaeological Importance (Forms of Notice, etc) Regulations 1984 and Appendix 2 hereof).

## Investigating authorities

The Secretary of State has power to appoint persons whom he considers to be competent to undertake archaeological investigations and to carry out other functions in AAIs pursuant to the 1979 Act (see section 34) as "investigating authorities". Where no person has been appointed by the Secretary of State the functions of the investigating authority are vested in English Heritage (as regards areas situated in England) or the Secretary of State in Wales. In practice appointments are likely to be limited to County Councils' archaeological officers, academic institutions and appropriately qualified and experienced independent organisations.

Where an operations notice is served, the investigating authority has a right to enter the site and any land giving access to the site at any reasonable time for the purposes of:

- inspecting the site (including buildings or other structures on the site) with a view to recording matters of archaeological or historic interest and determining whether or not it would be desirable to carry out excavations; and
- observing any operations carried out on the site with a view to examining and recording any objects or other material of archaeological or historic interest discovered during those operations.

Upon receipt of an operations notice, the investigating authority also have the right to excavate the site if, within the period of four weeks of receipt of the operations notice, the authority:

- serves notice in the prescribed form upon the developer informing it of the authority's intention to excavate;
- serves a copy of that notice on any council served with the Operations Notice and the Secretary of State; and
- where the site is in England, serves a copy of that notice on English Heritage.

If these procedural steps are followed, the investigating authority has a period of four months and two weeks to carry out its investigations such period commencing:

- at the end of the period of six weeks beginning with the date the Operations Notice was served; or
- where the operations are to be carried out after site clearance, the date of receipt of the notification of the clearance of the site (or the six week period mentioned above whichever is the later); or
- any earlier date agreed between the investigating authority and the developer.

(See section 38(4) of the 1979 Act.)

Where the investigating authority has given notice of its intention to excavate and a period of six weeks commencing with the date of service of the operations notice has expired, the Authority has the right to carry out excavations within the are of the site for the purposes of archaeological investigation provided that the authority does not obstruct the execution of clearance or other operations (section 38(5)).

The Secretary of State has the power to make directions imposing conditions upon the investigating authority as to the manner in which it exercises its powers (subject to prior consultation with English Heritage).

If a body possessing compulsory purchase powers notifies the investigating authority that it proposes to carry out or authorise the carrying out of operations, the investigating authority has a right to enter at any reasonable time for the purpose of inspecting the site and recording any matters of interest (section 39(1) of the 1979 Act). Such rights cease to have effect following the expiry of one month beginning with the date on which they were first exercised.

In addition to the powers of the investigating authority, where an Operations Notice has been served, any person authorised in writing by the Secretary of State or the Royal Commission on Historical Monuments may also enter the site at any reasonable time for the purpose of inspecting the site and any building or other structure thereon and recording matters of archaeological or historic interest (see section 40 of the 1979 Act).

These powers of entry do not extend to any buildings or parts of buildings occupied as a dwellinghouse unless the occupiers give their consent (except where entry is required for the purposes of survey or valuation in connection with a compensation claim) (see sections 43 and 44 of the 1979 Act).

## Other AAI offences

Any person using a metal detector within an AAI without the written consent of English Heritage or the Secretary of State will be guilty of an offence and liable on summary conviction to a fine not exceeding £200 (section 42(1) of the 1979 Act). Furthermore any person who, without such written consent, removes any object of archaeological or historic interest which he has discovered by using a metal detector will be guilty of a further offence triable in either the magistrates' court or the Crown Court. The maximum penalty in the magistrates' court is a fine not exceeding the statutory maximum (currently £5,000). There is no limitation upon the maximum fine upon conviction in the Crown Court (section 42(3)).

## Compensation

Where damage has been caused to land or chattels following exercise of any of the statutory rights of entry mentioned above any person interested in the land or chattels may recover compensation from the Secretary of State or English Heritage or other authority by or on whose behalf the power was exercised (section 46(1) of the 1979 Act). Where damage has been caused by an investigating authority in respect of an AAI compensation is recoverable from English Heritage or the Secretary of State. Any disputed issues as to compensation should be referred to the Lands Tribunal who will determine such questions in accordance with the Land Compensation Act 1961.

## Crown land and ecclesiastical property

Similar Crown exemption provisions are contained in the 1979 Act as regards scheduled monuments and AAI's as are set out in the 1990 Act relating to listed buildings – that is to say monuments on Crown land may be scheduled. The other general restrictions and powers contained in the 1979 Act shall apply to Crown land and anything done thereon:

- otherwise than acts carried out by or on behalf of the Crown; and
- not so as to affect any interest of the Crown.

No powers are exercisable under the Act and no interest may be compulsorily acquired except with the consent of the appropriate "Crown Authority" – that is to say:

- in the case of land belonging to Her Majesty in right of the Crown and forming part of the Crown Estate – the Crown Estate Commissioners;
- in relation to any other land belonging to Her Majesty in right of the Crown – the Government Department having management of that land;
- in relation to land belonging to Her Majesty in right of the Duchy of Lancaster – the Chancellor of the Duchy;
- in relation to land belonging to the Duchy of Cornwall – such person as the Duke of Cornwall or the possessor for the time being of the Duchy so appoints; and
- in the case of land belonging to a government department or held in trust for Her Majesty for the purposes of the government department – that department.

Any question arising as to which authority is the appropriate authority shall be referred to the Treasury whose decision shall be final. The term "Government Department" includes any "Minister of the Crown". (See section 50 of the 1979 Act.)

As regards ecclesiastical property, (*i.e.* land belonging to an ecclesiastical benefice of the Anglican Church, or being or forming part of a Church subject to the jurisdiction of a Bishop of any Anglican diocese or the site of such a Church, or being or forming part of a burial ground subject to such jurisdiction) where any notice is required to be served on the owner a like notice must also be served on the Church Commissioners. Where the freehold interest of any ecclesiastical property is in abeyance it shall be treated as being vested in the Church Commissioners. Where any compensation is payable as regards refusal or withdrawal of scheduled monument consent or damage to land or chattels such sums shall be paid to the Church Commissioners to be applied as if they were proceeds of sale (see section 51 of the 1979 Act).

## General policy considerations and their relationship with the planning system

General national policy guidance is set out in Planning Policy Guidance Note 16 Archaeology and Planning ("PPG 16"). The following themes are stressed:

- archaeological remains are a finite and non-renewable resource – appropriate management is essential to ensure that they survive in good condition;
- such remains are valuable for their own sake and for their role in education, leisure and tourism;
- there is a presumption in favour of physical preservation where nationally important remains whether scheduled or not (writer's emphasis) and their settings are affected by proposed development;
- appropriate planning policies in development plans and the implementation of those policies through development control decisions is especially important;
- development plans should reconcile the need for development with the interests of conservation including archaeology;
- UDPs and local plans should include policies for the protection, enhancement and preservation of sites and their settings;
- remains which are identified and scheduled as being nationally important should normally be earmarked for preservation in development plans (this may apply to unscheduled remains of more than local importance);
- in determining planning applications the desirability of preserving ancient monuments (scheduled are not) and their setting is a material consideration;
- development plans should not include policies requiring developers to finance archaeological work in exchange for planning permission;
- where preservation in situ is not justified and development should proceed notwithstanding that it will result in destruction of the remains, it is reasonable for the LPA to satisfy itself prior to granting permission that the developers

will make proper provision for the excavation and recording of any remains prior to the commencement of the development.

# Archaeology and planning conditions

General government guidance upon the use of planning conditions (Department of the Environment Circular 11/95) confirms the general approach adopted by planning law and policy to the effect that where scheduled ancient monuments and archaeological areas are protected by the provisions of the 1979 Act it should not be the role of planning conditions to duplicate such protection. However, where development requiring planning permission may affect a monument which has not been scheduled or which may affect land of archaeological interest but not formally designated under the 1979 Act the LPA may impose conditions to protect the monument or insure that appropriate access is granted to a nominated archaeologist who may observe works or carry out an investigation. Such conditions should comply with the usual policy requirement relating to planning conditions, *i.e.* they must be necessary, fair, reasonable and practicable. They must also be relevant to planning and to the development in question. Such advice is repeated in Paragraphs 29 and 30 of PPG16. Circular 11/95 suggests the following alternative model conditions:

- no development shall take place until fencing has been erected, in a manner to be agreed with the local planning authority, about [*insert name of monument*]; and no work shall take place within the area inside that fencing without the consent of the local planning authority;
- the developer shall afford access at all reasonable times to an archaeologist nominated by the local planning authority and shall allow him to observe the excavations and record items of interest and finds. *Conditions should not require work to be held up while archaeological investigation takes place, although some developers may be willing to give such facilities*;
- no development shall take place within the area indicated (this would be the area of archaeological interest) until the applicant or their agents or successors in title, has secured the implementation of a programme of archaeological work in

accordance with a written scheme of investigation which has been submitted by the applicant and approved in writing by the local planning authority. *Developers will wish to ensure that in drawing up the scheme, the timetable for the investigation is included within the details of the agreed scheme;*

# Relevant Organisations and Statutory Bodies

Department of Culture Media and
Sport
2-4 Cockspur Street
London SW16 5H
Tel: 020 7211 6000
Fax: 020 7211 6382

Department of the Environment,
Transport and the Regions
Eland House
Bressenden Place
London SW1E 5DU
Tel: 020 7944 3000

English Heritage
23 Savile Row
London W1X 1AB
Tel: 020 7973 3000
Fax: 020 7973 3001

National Monuments
Record Centre
Kemble Drive
Swindon SN2 2G2
Tel: 01793 414700
Fax: 01793 414924

Royal Commission on Ancient and
Historical Monuments in Wales
Crown Buildings
Aberystwyth
Dyfed SY23 2HP
Tel: 01970 624 381/2

Commission for Architecture and the
Built Environment
The Tower Building
11 York Road
London SE1 7HX
Tel: 020 7960 2400
Fax: 020 7960 2444
e-mail: enquiries@cabe.org.uk

Local Government Association
Chapter House
26 Chapter Street
London SW1P 4ND
Tel: 020 7000 000
Fax: 020 7000 000

Association of London Government
36 Old Queen Street
London SW1H 9JF
Tel 020 7222 7799
Fax: 020 7799 2339

Association of Conservation Officers
PO Box 301
Brighton
Sussex BN2 IBQ

Association of County
Archaeological Officers
Planning Department
Essex County Council
County Hall
Chelmsford
Essex CM1 1LF
Tel: 01245 492211

English Historic Town Forum
The Huntingdon Centre
The Vineyards
The Paragon
Bath BA1 5NA
Tel: 01225 469157

Garden History Society
Station House
Church Lane
Wickwar
Wotton-under-Edge
Gloucestershire GL12 8NB
Tel: 01454 294 888

Civic Trust
17 Charlton House Terrace
London SW1Y 5AW
Tel: 020 7930 0914

Architectural Heritage Fund
27 John Adam Street
London WC2N 6HX
Tel: 020 7925 1099

United Kingdom Association of
Building Preservation Trusts
c/o The Architectural Heritage Fund
27 John Adam Street
London WC2N 6HX

Theatres Trust
Doric House
22 Charing Cross Road
London WC2H OHR
Tel: 020 7836 8591

International Council on Monuments
and Sites
10 Barley Mow Passage
Chiswick
London W4 4PH
Tel: 020 7994 6477

Council for British Archaeology
Bowes Morrell House
111 Walmgate
York YO 1 2UA
Tel: 01904 671417

Georgian Group
37 Spital Square
London E1 6DTY
Tel: 020 7377 1722

Victorian Society
1 Priory Gardens
Bedford Park
London WR8 1TT
Tel: 020 8994 1019

Twentieth Century Society
58 Crescent Lane
London SW4 9PU
Tel: 020 7793 9898

Joint Committee of the National
Amenity Societies
St Ann's Vestry Hall
2 Church Entry
London EC4V 5AB
Tel: 020 7236 3934

Society for the Protection of Ancient Buildings
37 Spital Square
London E1 6DY
Tel: 020 7377 1644

Ancient Monuments Society
St Ann's Vestry Hall
2 Church Entry
London EC4V 5AB

**Religious Denominations Exempted**
General Synod of the Church of England
Church House
Great Smith Street
London SW1P 3NZ
Tel: 020 7222 9011

Methodist Church
Property Division
Central Buildings
Oldham Street
Manchester M11 JQ
Tel: 0161 236 5194

United Reformed Church
c/o Towns, Needham and Co
Solicitors
6/8 Albert Road
Levenshulme
Manchester M19 3PJ
Tel: 0161 225 0040

Roman Catholic Church
Catholic Bishops'
Conference of England and Wales
Allington House (1st Floor)
136/147 Victoria Street
London SW1E 5LD
Tel: 020 7630 8221

Baptist Union of Great Britain
c/o Baptist Union
Corporation Ltd
PO Box 44
129 Broadway
Didcot
Oxfordshire OX11 8RT

**Other Relevant Church of England Bodies**

Council for the Care of Churches
83 London Wall
London EC2M 5NA

Cathedrals Fabric Commission for England
83 London Wall
London EC2M 5NA
Tel: 020 7638 0971

Church Commissioners for England
1 Millbank
London SW1P 3JZ
Tel: 020 7222 7010

Advisory Board for Redundant Churches
Fielden House
Litttle College Street
London SW1P 3SH
Tel: 020 7222 9603

*Appendix 2*

# Town and Country · Planning (Trees) · Regulations 1999

**MODEL FORM OF TREE PRESERVATION ORDER**

Town and Country Planning Act 1990

**The [title of Order (including year)]**

The [*name of Council*], in exercise of the powers conferred on them by sections 198, [201] and 203 of the Town and Country Planning Act 1990 hereby make the following Order–

**Citation** 1. This Order may be cited as the [*title of Order (including year)*].

**Interpretation** 2. In this Order "the authority" means the [*name of Council making the Order*] and unless the context otherwise requires, any reference in this Order to a numbered sectionis a reference to the sectionso numbered in the Town and Country Planning Act 1990.

**[Application of section 201**

3. The authority hereby direct that section 201 (provisional tree preservation orders) shall apply to this Order and, accordingly, this Order shall take effect provisionally on (*insert date*).]

**Prohibited acts in relation to trees**

4. Without prejudice to subsections (6) and (7) of section 198 (power to make tree preservation orders)(1) [or subsection (3) of section 200 (orders affecting land where Forestry Commissioners interested)], and subject to article 5, no person shall–

(a)    cut down, top, lop, uproot, wilfully damage or wilfully destroy; or

(b)    cause or permit the cutting down, topping, lopping, uprooting, wilful damage or wilful destruction of, any tree specified in Schedule 1 to this Order or comprised in a group of trees or in a woodland so specified, except with the consent of the authority and, where such consent is given subject to conditions, in accordance with those conditions.

**Exemptions**

5. [1]Nothing in article 4 shall prevent

(a) the cutting down, topping, lopping or uprooting of a tree by or at the request of a statutory undertaker, where the land on which the tree is situated is operational land of the statutory undertaker and the work is necessary:

(i) in the interests of the safe operation of the undertaking;

(ii) in connection with the inspection, repair or renewal of any sewers, mains, pipes, cables or other apparatus of the statutory undertaker; or

(iii) to enable the statutory undertaker to carry out development permitted by or under the Town and Country Planning (General Permitted Development) Order 1995;

(b) the cutting down, topping, lopping or uprooting of a tree cultivated for the production of fruit in the course of a business or trade where such work is in the interests of that business or trade;

(c) the pruning, in accordance with good horticultural practice, of any tree cultivated for the production of fruit;

(d)   the cutting down, topping, lopping or uprooting of a tree where that work is required to enable a person to implement a planning permission (other than an outline planning permission or, without prejudice to paragraph (a)(iii), a permission granted by or under the Town and Country Planning (General Permitted Development) Order 1995) granted on an application under Part III of the Act, or deemed to have been granted (whether for the purposes of that Part or otherwise);

(e)   the cutting down, topping, lopping or uprooting of a tree by or at the request of the Environment Agency to enable the Agency to carry out development permitted by or under the Town and Country Planning (General Development Order) 1995;

(f)   the cutting down, topping, lopping or uprooting of a tree by or at the request of a drainage body where that tree interferes, or is likely to interfere, with the exercise of any of the functions of that body in relation to the maintenance, improvement or construction of watercourses or of drainage works, and for this purpose "drainage body" and "drainage" have the same meanings as in the Land Drainage Act 1991; or

---

1 Subsection (6) of section 198 exempts from the application of tree preservation orders the cutting down, uprooting, topping or lopping or lopping trees which are dying, dead or have become dangerous, or the undertaking of those acts in compliance with obligations imposed by or under an Act of Parliament or so far as may be necessary for the prevention or abatement of a nuisance. Subsection (7) of that section makes section 198 subject to section 39(2) of the Housing and Planning Act 1986 and section 14 of the Forestry Act 1967.

(g)    without prejudice to section198(6)(b), the felling or lopping of a tree or the cutting back of its roots by or at the request of, or in accordance with a notice served by, a licence holder under paragraph 9 of Schedule 4 to the Electricity Act 1989.

(2)    In paragraph (1), "statutory undertaker" means any of the following-:

■ a person authorised by any enactment to carry on any railway, light railway, tramway, road transport, water transport, canal, inland navigation, dock, harbour, pier or lighthouse undertaking, or any undertaking for the supply of hydraulic power,

■ a relevant airport operator (within the meaning of Part V of the Airports Act 1986),

■ the holder of a licence under section 6 of the Electricity Act 1989,

■ a public gas transporter,

■ the holder of a licence under section 7 of the Telecommunications Act 1984 to whom the telecommunications code (within the meaning of that Act) is applied,

■ a water or sewerage undertaker,

■ the Civil Aviation Authority or a body acting on behalf of that Authority,

■ the Post Office.

### Applications for consent under the Order

6.    An application for consent to the cutting down, topping, lopping or uprooting of any tree in respect of which this Order is for the time being in force shall be made in writing to the authority and shall--

(a) identify the tree or trees to which it relates (if necessary, by reference to a plan);

(b) specify the work for which consent is sought; and

(c) contain a statement of the applicant's reasons for making the application.

### Application of provisions of the Town and Country Planning Act 1990

7.    (1) The provisions of the Town and Country Planning Act 1990 relating to registers, applications, permissions and appeals mentioned in column (1) of Part I of Schedule 2 to this Order shall have effect, in relation to consents under this Order and applications for such consent, subject to the adaptations and modifications mentioned in column (2).

(2)    **The provisions referred to in paragraph (1), as so adapted and modified, are set out in Part II of that Schedule.**

### Directions as to replanting

8.    (1) Where consent is granted under this Order for the felling in the

course of forestry operations of any part of a woodland area, the authority may give to the owner of the land on which that part is situated ("the relevant land") a direction in writing specifying the manner in which and the time within which he shall replant the relevant land.

(2) Where a direction is given under paragraph (1) and trees on the relevant land are felled (pursuant to the consent), the owner of that land shall replant it in accordance with the direction.

(3) A direction under paragraph (1) may include requirements as to–
  (a) species;
  (b) number of trees per hectare;
  (c) the preparation of the relevant land prior to the replanting;
and
(d) the erection of fencing necessary for the protection of the newly planted trees.

## Compensation

9.    (1) If, on a claim under this article, a person establishes that loss or damage has been caused or incurred in consequence of–-
      (a) the refusal of any consent required under this Order; or
      (b) the grant of any such consent subject to conditions, he shall, subject to paragraphs (3) and (4), be entitled to compensation from the authority.

(2) No claim, other than a claim made under paragraph (3), may be made under this article–
      (a) if more than 12 months has elapsed since the date of the authority's decision or, where such a decision is the subject of an appeal to the Secretary of State, the date of the final determination of the appeal; or
      (b) if the amount in respect of which the claim would otherwise have been made is less than £500.

(3) Where the authority refuse consent under this Order for the felling in the course of forestry operations of any part of a woodland area, they shall not be required to pay compensation to any person other than the owner of the land; and such compensation shall be limited to an amount equal to any depreciation in the value of the trees which is attributable to deterioration in the quality of the timber in consequence of the refusal.

(4) In any other case, no compensation shall be payable to a person–

(a) for loss of development value or other diminution in the value of the land;

(b) for loss or damage which, having regard to the statement of reasons submitted in accordance with article 6(c) and any documents or other evidence submitted in support of any such statement, was not reasonably foreseeable when consent was refused or was granted subject to conditions;

(c) for loss or damage reasonably foreseeable by that person and attributable to his failure to take reasonable steps to avert the loss or damage or to mitigate its extent; or

(d) for costs incurred in appealing to the Secretary of State against the refusal of any consent required under this Order or the grant of any such consent subject to conditions.

(5) Subsections (3) to (5) of section 11 (terms of compensation on refusal of licence) of the Forestry Act 1967 shall apply to the assessment of compensation under paragraph (3) as it applies to the assessment of compensation where a felling licence is refused under section 10 (application for felling licence and decision of Commissioners thereon) of that Act as if for any reference to a felling licence there were substituted a reference to a consent required under this Order and for the reference to the Commissioners there were substituted a reference to the authority.

(6) In this article–

"development value" means an increase in value attributable to the prospect of development; and, in relation to any land, the development of it shall include the clearing of it; and

"owner" has the meaning given to it by section 34 of the Forestry Act 1967.

**[Application to trees to be planted pursuant to a condition**
[10.] In relation to the tree[s] identified in the first column of Schedule 1 by the letter "C", being [a tree] [trees] to be planted pursuant to a condition (being a condition imposed under paragraph (a) of section 197 (planning permission to include appropriate provision for preservation and planting of trees)), this Order takes effect as from the time when [that tree is planted] [those trees are planted].]

**[Orders made by virtue of section 300**
[11.] This Order takes effect in accordance with subsection(3) of section 300 (tree preservation orders in anticipation of disposal of Crown land).]

Dated this [ ] day of [insert month and year]
[*if the Council's Standing Orders require* the sealing *of such* documents:]

[The Common Seal of the [insert name of Council] was hereunto affixed in the presence of

..................................................................]

[*if* the Council's *Standing Orders do not require* the sealing *of such* documents:]
[Signed on behalf of the [insert name of Council] authorised by the Council to sign

.............................................................
Authorised on that behalf]

### [CONFIRMATION OF ORDER]

[This Order was confirmed by the [insert name of Council] without modification on the [ ] day of [insert month and year]] OR [This Order was confirmed by the [insert name of Council, subject to the modifications indicated by [state how *indicated*], *on* the [     ] day of [insert month and year]

.............................................................
Authorised by the Council to sign in that behalf]

### [DECISION NOT TO CONFIRM ORDER]

[A decision not to confirm this Order was taken by [insert name *of* Council on the [     ] day of [insert month and year]

.............................................................
Authorised by the Council to sign in that behalf]

### [VARIATION OF ORDER]

[This Order was varied by the [insert name of Council on the [ ] day of [insert *month and year*] under the reference number [insert reference number of the variation order]

.............................................................
Authorised by the Council to sign in that behalf]

### [REVOCATION OF ORDER]

[This Order was revoked by the [insert name *of* Council] on the [ ] day of [insert *month and year*] under the reference number [insert reference number of the revocation order]

.............................................................
Authorised by the Council to sign in that behalf]

# Schedule 1

## Specification of trees

Trees specified individually
(encircled in black on the map)

| Reference on map | Description | Situation |
|---|---|---|
| [T1] | [ash] | [complete if necessary to specify more precisely the position of the trees] |

Trees specified by reference to an area
(within a dotted black line on the map)

| Reference on map | Description | Situation |
|---|---|---|
| [Al] | [trees (of whatever species) within the precisely area marked A1 on the map] | [complete if necessary to specify more precisely the position of the trees] |
| [A2] | [the ash, beech, larch and oak trees within precisely the area marked A2 on the map] | [complete if necessary to specify more precisely the position of the trees] |

### Groups of trees
(within a broken black line on the map)

| Reference on map | Description (including number of trees in the group) | Situation |
|---|---|---|
| [G 1 ] | [2 ash trees, 3 elm trees and 3 oak trees] | [complete if necesary to specify mroe precisely the position of the trees] |

### Woodlands
(within a continuous black line on the map)

| Reference on map | Description | Situation |
|---|---|---|
| [w1] | [mixed hardwoods (mainly      )] | [complete if necessary to specify more precisely the position of the trees] |
| [W2] | [mixed conifers and deciduous trees (mainly      )] | |

# Schedule 2

## PART I

## Provisions of the Town and Country Planning Act 1990 Applied with adaptations for modifications

| Provision of the Town and Country Planning Act 1990 | Adaptation or Modification |
|---|---|
| Section 69 (registers) | (a)  In subsection(1) – <br><br>(i) omit– <br>", in such manner as may be prescribed by a Development order," <br>"such" in the second place where it appears, <br>And <br>"as may be so prescribed"; and <br><br>(ii) substitute "matters relevant to tree preservation <br>orders made by the authority "for applications for planning permission". <br><br>(b)  In subsection(2) – <br><br>(i) after "contain "insert", as regards each such Order"; and <br>(ii) for paragraphs (a) and (b) substitute <br><br>(a) details of every application under the Order and of the authority's decision (if Any) in relation to each such application, and <br>(b) a statement as to the subject-matter of Every appeal under the order and of the Date and nature of the Secretary of State's determination of it." |

|  |  |
|---|---|
|  | (c) Omit subsections (3) and (4) (as required by section 198(4)). |
| Section 70 (determination of applications: general considerations) | (a) In subsection(1)-<br>(i) substitute-<br><br>"Subject to subsections (1A) and (1 B), where"<br>For "Where";<br><br>"the authority" for "a local planning authority";"consent under a tree preservation order" for "planning permission" where those words first Appear; and<br><br>"consent under the order" for "planning Permission" in both of the other places where Those words appear;<br><br>(ii) after "think fit", insert<br><br>"(including conditions limiting the duration of The consent or requiring the replacement of Trees)"; and<br><br>(iii) omit "subject to sections 91 and 92,".<br><br>(c) After subsection(1) insert<br><br>"(1A) Where an application relates to an area of Woodland, the authority shall grant consent so far as accords with the practice of good forestry, unless they are satisfied that the granting of consent would fail to secure the maintenance of the special character of the woodland or the woodland character of the area.<br><br>(1 B) Where the authority grant consent for the Felling of trees in a woodland area they shall not Impose conditions requiring replacement where such felling is carried |

| | |
|---|---|
| | out in the course of forestry operations (but may give directions for securing replanting).". <br><br> (d) Omit subsections (2) and (3). |
| Section75 (effect of planning permission) | (a) In subsection (1) substitute– <br><br> (i)"Any" for the words from "Without" to "any"; <br> (ii) "consent under a tree preservation order" for "planning permission to develop land"; <br> (ii)"the consent" for "the permission"; and <br> (iv) "the land to which the order relates" for "the land". <br><br> (b) Omit subsections (2) and (3). |
| Section78 (right to appeal against planning decisions and failure to take such decisions) | (a) In subsection(1) substitute– <br><br> (i) "the authority" for "a local planning authority"; <br> (ii) "consent under a tree preservation order" for "planning permission" in the first place where those words appear; <br> (iii) "consent under such an order" for "planning Permission" in the second place where those words appear; <br> (iv) for paragraph (c) substitute– <br><br> "(c) give a direction under a tree preservation order, or refuse an application for any consent, agreement or approval of that authority required by such a direction; or <br><br> (d) fail to determine any such application as is referred to in paragraphs (a) to (c) within the period of 8 weeks beginning with the date on which the application was received by the authority". |

(b) Omit subsection(2).

(c) In subsection(3) for "served within such time and in such manner as may be prescribed by a development order." substitute–

"in writing addressed to the Secretary of State, Specifying the grounds on which the appeal is made; and such notice shall be served–

(a) in respect of a matter mentioned in any of Paragraphs (a) to (c) of subsection(1), within the period of 28 days from the receipt of Notification of the authority's decision or Direction or within such longer period as the Secretary of State may allow;

(b) in respect of such a failure as is mentioned in Paragraph (d) of that subsection, at any time after the expiration of the period mentioned in that paragraph, but if the authority have Informed the applicant that the application has been refused, or granted subject to conditions, before an appeal has been made, an appeal may only be made against that refusal or grant."

(d) For subsection(4), substitute"(4) The appellant shall serve on the authority a copy of the notice mentioned in subsection(3)."

(e) For subsection(5), substitute–

"(5) For the purposes of the application of section

| | |
|---|---|
| | 79(1), in relation to an appeal made under subsection(1)(d), it shall be assumed that the authority decided to refuse the application in question." |
| Section 79 (determination of appeals) | (a) In subsections (1) and (2), substitute "the authority" for "the local planning authority". <br> (b) Omit subsection(3). <br> (c) In subsection(4), substitute- <br><br> (i) "section70(1), (1 A) and (1 B)" for "sections 70, 72(1) and (5), 73 and 73A and Part I of Schedule 5"; <br> (ii) "consent under a tree preservation order" for "planning permission"; and <br> (iii) "the authority" for "the local planning authority And a development order may apply, with or Without modifications, to such an appeal any Requirements imposed by a development order by virtue of sections 65 or 71." <br><br> (d) Omit subsections (6) and (6A). <br><br> (e) In subsection(7), omit the words after "section78". |

# Part II

## Provisions of the Town and Country Planning Act 1990, as adapted and modified by Part I

The following provisions of the Town and Country Planning Act 1990, as adapted and modified by Part I of this Schedule, apply in relation to consents, and applications for consent, under this Order.

## Section 69

(1) Every local planning authority shall keep a register containing information with respect to matters relevant to tree preservation orders made by the authority.
(2) The register shall contain, as regards each such order-

(a) details of every application under the order and of the authority's decision (if any) in relation to each such application, and
(b) a statement as to the subject-matter of every appeal under the order and of the date and nature of the Secretary of State's determination of it.

(5) Every register kept under this sectionshall be available for inspection by the public at all reasonable hours.

## Section 70

(1) Subject to subsections (1A) and (1B), where an application is made to the authority for consent under a tree preservation order–

(a) they may grant consent under the order, either unconditionally or subject to such conditions as they think fit (including conditions limiting the duration of the consent or requiring the replacement of trees); or
(b) they may refuse consent under the order.

(1A) Where an application relates to an area of woodland, the authority shall grant consent so far as accords with the practice of good forestry, unless they are satisfied that the granting of consent would fail to secure the maintenance of the special character of the woodland or the woodland character of the area.

(1 B) Where the authority grant consent for the felling of trees in a woodland area they shall not impose conditions requiring replacement where such felling is carried out in the course of forestry operations (but may give directions for securing replanting).

## Section 75

Any grant of consent under a tree preservation order shall (except in so far as the consent otherwise provides) ensure for the benefit of the land to which the order relates and of all persons for the time being interested in it.

## Section 78

(1) Where the authority–

(a) refuse an application for consent under a tree preservation order or grant it subject to conditions;

(b)refuse an application for any consent, agreement or approval of that authority required by a condition imposed on a grant of consent under such an order or grant it subject to conditions;

(c) give a direction under a tree preservation order, or refuse an application for any consent, agreement or approval of that authority required by such a direction; or

(d) fail to determine any such application as is referred to in paragraphs (a) to (c) within the period of 8 weeks beginning with the date on which the application was received by the authority, the applicant may by notice appeal to the Secretary of State.

(3) Any appeal under this sectionshall be made by notice in writing addressed to the Secretary of State, specifying the grounds on which the appeal is made; and such notice shall be served–

(a) in respect of a matter mentioned in any of paragraphs (a) to (c) of subsection(1), within the period of 28 days from the receipt of notification of the authority's decision or direction or within such longer period as the Secretary of State may allow;

(b) in respect of such a failure as is mentioned in paragraph (d) of that subsection, at any time after the expiration of the period mentioned in that paragraph, but if the authority have informed the applicant that the application has been refused, or granted subject to conditions, before an appeal has been made, an appeal may only be made against that refusal or grant.

(4) The appellant shall serve on the authority a copy of the notice mentioned in subsection(3).

(5) For the purposes of the application of section79(1), in relation to an appeal made under subsection(1)(d), it shall be assumed that the authority decided to refuse the application in question.


## Section 79

(1) On an appeal under section 78 the Secretary of State may–

(a) allow or dismiss the appeal, or

(b) reverse or vary any part of the decision of the authority (whether the appeal relates to that part of it or not),and may deal with the application as if it had been made to him in the first instance.

(2) Before determining an appeal under section 78 the Secretary of State shall, if either the appellant or the authority so wish, give each of them an opportunity of appearing before and being heard by a person appointed by the Secretary of State for the purpose.

(4) Subject to subsection(2), the provisions of section 70(1), (1A) and (1B) shall apply, with any necessary modifications, in relation to an appeal to the Secretary of State under section 78 as they apply in relation to an application for consent under a tree preservation order which falls to be determined by the authority.

(5) The decision of the Secretary of State on such an appeal shall be final.

(7) Schedule 6 applies to appeals under section 78.

*Appendix 3*

# Form of Hedgerow Removal Notice

## The Environment Act 1995

## The Hedgerows Regulations 1997

To: (Name and address of
Local planning authority)

...............................................................................................................

...............................................................................................................

1. From: (Name and address of person giving the notice ................................

...............................................................................................................

...............................................................................................................

1. I give you notice under regulation 5(1)(a) of the above regulations that I propose to remove the [stretch(es) of] hedgerow(s) indicated on the attached plan. *(If possible, please provide a plan to a scale of 1:2500. A different scale can be used so long as it shows clearly the location and length of the hedgerows that you wish to remove.)*

2. The reasons why I propose to remove it/them are the following:

3. Of the [stretch(es) of] hedgerow(s) indicated, those marked with an "X" were planted less than 30 years ago. Evidence of the date of planting is attached.

4. I am/We are the owner(s) of the freehold title of the land concerned.

OR (please delete as appropriate)
I am/We are the tenant(s) of the agricultural holding concerned.

OR (please delete as appropriate)
I am/We are the tenant(s) under the farm business tenancy concerned

OR (please delete as appropriate)
I am/act for the utility operator concerned.

.........................................          .....................................
(Signature of person giving notice)          (Date)

# Forms Prescribed by the Operations in Areas of · Archaelogical Importance · (Forms of Notice, etc) Regulations 1984

FORM OF NOTICE TO BE GIVEN BEFORE CARRYING OUT IN AN AREA OF ARCHAEOLOGICAL IMPORTANCE OPERATIONS WHICH DISTURB THE GROUND, FLOODING OPERATIONS, OR TIPPING OPERATIONS

OPERATIONS NOTICE

ANCIENT MONUMENTS AND ARCHAEOLOGICAL AREAS ACT 1979:
SECTION 35

(To be completed by or on behalf of the Developer (footnote 1) in BLOCK CAPITALS or typescript)

I/We,
Name:..............................................................................................
Address:
.........................................................................................................
.........................................................................................................
...
.........................................................................................................
....
Postcode: ..................................... Tel. No...........................................

hereby give notice of my/our intention to carry out the operations described below.

A certificate in accordance with section 35 of the Ancient Monuments and Archaeological Areas Act 1979 accompanies this notice.

I/We understand that if within six weeks of serving this notice I/we carry out or cause or permit to be carried out any operations referred to in this notice I/we may be guilty of an offence under section 35 of the 1979 Act.

### Particulars of proposed operations

1. Description of proposed operations (footnote 2):
2. The Site on which the operations are to be carried out:

*Name: (if any)* ...........................................................................................
*Address of Location:*.....................................................................................
*Ordnance Survey National Grid Reference:*.................................................

(NOTE: Where the extent of the site cannot be accurately identified from its address or location; a clear plan of the site of the operations should be provided.)

3. The date on which it is proposed to begin the operations:...........................
.......................................................................................................................
[4.Where the operations are to be carried out after clearance of the site (footnote 3) the Developer's estimated date for completion of the clearance operations (footnotes 4 and 5)............................................................................
......................................................................................................................]
Signature .................................... Date .....................................
on behalf of .........................................................................................*

*Where the notice is being given by an agent to whom correspondence should be sent, state the –*

Name of agent ..............................................................................................
Address of agent ..........................................................................................
......................................................................................................................
Postcode: .................................... Tel. No. .....................................


SERVICE OF THIS NOTICE

This notice is to be served on the district council or London borough council or where the site of the operations is within a National Park, the notice is to be served instead on the National Park authority or (as the case may be) on each district council or London borough council in whose are the site of the operations is wholly or partially situated except that where the site is partially within a National Park the notice is to be served on the National Park authority to the extent that the site is within its area except that where the developer is any such council or authority this notice shall be served on the Secretary of State at 2-4 Cockspur Street, London SW1Y 5DH (Buildings, Monuments & Sites Division) where the site is in England and at Cathays Park, Cardiff CF1 3HQ where the site is in Wales.

## Footnotes

1. "Developer" means any person carrying out or proposing to carry out any operations: (section 35(3) of the 1979 Act).
2. "Operations" means operations which disturb the ground; flooding operations; and tipping operations; (section 35(2) of the 1979 Act). "Flooding operations" means covering land with water or any other liquid or partially liquid substance; (section 61(1) of the 1979 Act). "Tipping operations" means tipping soil or spoil or depositing building or other materials or matter (including waste materials or refuse) on any land; (section 61(1) of the 1979 Act). A reference to operations on any land includes a reference to operations in, under or over the land in question; (section 41(1)(c) of the 1979 Act).
3. "Clearance of the site" means the demolition and removal of any existing building or other structure on the site and the removal of any other materials thereon so as to clear the surface of the land (but does not include the levelling of the surface or the removal of the materials from below the surface); (section 41(1)(d) of the 1979 Act).
4. "Clearance operations" means operations undertaken for the purpose of in connection with the clearance of any site, (section 41(1)(e) of the 1979 Act).
5. Immediately on completion of clearance of the site the developer must notify the investigating authority for the area of archaeological importance in question. The council will inform the developer of the name and address of that investigating authority.
6. It is not necessary to serve a notice in this form in a case where the Areas of Archaeological Importance (Notification of Operations) (Exemption) Order 1984 provides exemption for the proposed operations.

## Form of CERTIFICATE FOR THE PURPOSES OF SECTION 35 OF THE ANCIENT MONUMENTS AND ARCHAEOLOGICAL AREAS ACT 1979

### Certificate accompanying an operations notice

1. I/We, Name ...................................................................................................

Address .................................................................................................................

.................................................................................................................................

Postcode ........................................... Tel No .........................................

hereby certify that with regard to the accompanying operations notice dated .........

.................................................*(insert date)* given by or on behalf of

.............................*(insert name of the Developer in the operations notice)*:

relating to operations at ................................. (give particulars of the site of the proposed operations)

☐ (a) I/We have an interest in the site of the operations which (apart from any restrictions imposed by law) entitles me/us to carry out the operations in question; or

☐ (b) I/We have a right to enter on and take possession of the site of the operations under section 11(1) or (2) of the Compulsory Purchase Act 1965 (powers of entry on land subject to compulsory purchase); or

☐ (c) This certificate is issued by statutory undertakers entitled to carry out the operations in question by or under the following enactment
(footnote .........................................................(insert enactment).

*Tick the box which applies.*

Signed.................................... Date ...............................

on behalf of ...................................................................................
*Where the certificate is given by an agent to whom the correspondence should be sent, state the –*

Name of the agent .................................................................

Address of the agent .............................................................

...................................................................................................

Postcode .................................... Tel No .............................

2. (To be completed only where the person issuing this certificate is not the Developer)

I ..................................................... *(name of person issuing this certificate)* hereby state that I have authorised the Developer mentioned in the accompanying operations notice dated ...............................................
*(insert date of operations notice)* to carry out the operations referred to in that notice.

Signed ...................................................... *(Signature of the person issuing this Certificate)*
Date .........................................

NOTE: If any person issues a certificate which purports to comply with the requirements of this form and which contains a statement which he knows to be false or misleading in a material particular, or recklessly issues a certificate which purports to comply with these requirements and which contains a statement which is false or misleading in a material particular, he shall be guilty of an offence.

Footnote

"Enactment" includes an enactment in any local or private Act of Parliament, and order, rule, regulation, bye-law or scheme made under an Act of Parliament; (section 61(1) of the 1979 Act).

### FORM OF NOTICE TO BE GIVEN BY AN INVESTIGATING AUTHORITY OF ITS INTENTION TO EXCAVATE

### ANCIENT MONUMENTS AND ARCHAEOLOGICAL AREAS ACT 1979: SECTION 38(3)

### NOTICE OF INTENTION TO EXCAVATE

TO: .................................................................................

.................................................................................

.................................................... *Name and Address of Developer*


1. TAKE NOTICE that I/We ...............................................

.................................................................................

.................................................................................

*Name and address of investigating authority*

being [the investigating authority] [authorised by section 34(4)][(5)] of the Act to exercise the powers of the investigating authority] (footnote 1) for the area of archaeological importance in which is situated the site referred to in an operations notice dated ...................................*(insert date)* and served by you on the ............................................................. *council(s) (insert name of council(s))* on ...................................................... *(insert dateI)* intend, during the period set out in paragraph 2 below, to carry out excavations on that site for the purpose of archaeological investigation (footnote 2)

2. The period allowed for excavations is four months and two weeks beginning with–

(a)  .....................................................*(insert the date immediately following the end of the period of six weeks beginning with the dae of service of the operations notice on the council(s)*; or
(b) if later (and where relevant), the date of receipt by me/us of the notification of clearance of the site pursuant to section 35(7) of the 1979 Act; or
(c)  any earlier date agreed between us [such date being......... ...................]. *(If such a date has been agreed before the service of this notice it should be inserted here and (a) and (b) should be deleted; if no such date has been agreed delete words in square brackets).*

NOTE: in a case where (b) is relevant (operations to be carried out after clearance of the site) the investigating authority has the right to carry out excavations before the relevant period begins provided that the authority does not thereby obstruct the execution on the site by the developer of clearance or other operations to which section 35 of the 1979 Act does not apply (footnote 3)

3. An investigating authority may at any reasonable time enter the site and any land giving access to it for the purpose of exercising its right to excavate.

4. It may be an offence for any person to carry out operations to which the operations notice relates to a time when the investigating authority has a right to excavate the site.

Signed...................................... Date .......................................

on behalf of ...................…...................................................

SERVICE OF THIS NOTICE

This notice must be served on the developer before the end of four weeks beginning with the date of service of the operations notice on the Council; (section 38(3) of the 1979 Act). Copies of this notice are to be served upon, (1) the Council(s) served with the operations notice; (2) The Secretary of State (unless the functions of the investigating authority are for the time being exercised by him) at 2–4 Cockspur Street London SW1Y 5DH as respects a site in England and at Cathays Park, Cardiff CF1 3HQ as respects a site in Wales; and (3) the Historic Buildings and Monuments Commission for England (unless the investigating authority is for the time being that Commission), as respects a site in England.

Footnotes

1. Delete whichever is inapplicable.  The powers of an investigating authority are exercisable by any authority duly authorised to exercise those powers.  Where no authority is appointed, the powers of such an authority are exercisable by the Commission in the case of an area in England and the Secretary of State in the case of an area in Wales.
2. "Archaeological investigation" means any investigation of any land, objects or other material for the purpose of obtaining and recording any information of archaeological or historical interest and (without prejudice to the generality of the preceding provision) includes in the case of an archaeological investigation of any land –
(a)      any investigation for the purpose of discovering and revealing and (where appropriate) recovering and removing any objects or other material of archaeological or historical interest situated in, on or under the land; and
(b)      examining, testing, recording and preserving any such objects or material discovered during the course of any excavations or inspections carried out for the purpose of any such investigation, (section 6(4) of the 1979 Act).
3. Section 35 of the 1979 Act applies to operations which disturb the ground; flooding operations; and tipping operations but it does not apply to any of those operations carried out with the consent of the investigating authority or to any operations exempted by an order under section 37 of the Act.

# Principal Provisions of the
# ▪        1990 Act        ▪

## 1. Listing of buildings of special architectural interest

(1)     For the purposes of this Act and with a view to the guidance of local planning authorities in the performance of their functions under this Act and the principal Act in relation to building of special architectural or historic interest, the Secretary of State shall compile a list of such buildings, or approve with or without modifications, such list compiled by the Historic Buildings and Monuments Commission for England (in this Act referred to as "the Commission") or by other persons or bodies of persons, and may amend any lists so compiled or approved.

(2)     The Secretary of State shall not approve any list compiled by the Commission if the list contains any building situated outside England.

(3)     In considering whether to include a building in a list compiled or approved under this section, the Secretary of State may take into account not only the building itself but also –

(a) in any respect in which its exterior contributes to the architectural or historic interest of any group of buildings of which it forms a part; and

(b) the desirability of preserving, on the grounds of its architectural or historic interest, any feature of the building consisting of a man-made object or structure fixed to the building or forming part of the land and comprised in the curtilage of the building.

(4)     Before compiling, approving (with or without modifications) or amending any list under this sectionthe Secretary of State shall consult –

(a) in relation to buildings which are situated within England, with the Commission; and

(b) with such other persons or bodies of persons as appear to him appropriate as having special knowledge of, or interest in, buildings of architectural or historic interest.

(5)    In this Act "listed building" means a building which is for the time being included in a list compiled or approved by the Secretary of State under this section; and for the purposes of this Act –
    (a) any object or structure fixed to the building;
    (b) any object or structure within the curtilage of the building which, although not fixed to the building, forms part of the land and has done so since before July 1, 1948,

shall be treated as part of the building.

(6)    Schedule 1 shall have effect for the purpose of making provision as to treatment of listed buildings formerly subject to building preservations orders.

# 3. Temporary listing: building preservation notices

(1)    If it appears to a local planning authority in Wales, or a local planning authority in England who are not a county planning authority, that the building in their area which is not a listed building –
    (a) is of special architectural historic interest; and
    (b) is in danger of demolition or of alteration in such a way as to affect its character as a list building of such interest,

they may serve on the owner and occupier of the building a notice (in this Act referred to as a "building preservation notice").

(2)    A building preservation notice served by a local planning authority shall
    (a) state that the building appears to them to be of special architectural interest and that they have requested the Secretary of State to consider including it in a list compiled or approved under Section1; and
    (b) explain the effect of sub-sections (3)to(5) and Schedule 2.
(3) A building preservation notice –
    (a) shall come into force as soon as it has been served on both the owner and occupier of the building to which it relates; and
    (b) subject to sub-section (4), shall remain in force for six months from the date when it is served or, as the case may be, last served.
(4) A building preservation notice shall cease to be in force if the Secretary of State –
    (a) includes a building in a list compiled or approved under Section1, or
    (b) notifies the local planning authority in writing that he does not intend to do so.

(5) While a building preservation notice is in force with respect to a building, the provisions of this Act (other than section 59 [*acts causing or likely to result in damage to listed – see Chap* 2]) and the principal Act shall have effect in relation to the building as if it were a listed building.

(6) If, following the service of a building preservation notice, the Secretary of State notifies the local planning authority that he does not propose to include the building in a list compiled or approved under Section1, the authority shall immediately give notice of that decision to the owner and occupier of the building.

(7) Following such a notification by the Secretary of State no further building preservation notice in respect of the building shall be served by the local planning authority within the period of 12 months beginning with the date of the notification.

(8) The Commission shall, as respects any London Borough, have concurrently with the council of that borough the functions of a local planning authority under this section and references to the local planning authority shall be construed accordingly.

# 6. Issue of certificate that building not intended to be listed

(1)    Where –
          (a) application has been made for planning permission for any development involving the alteration, extension of demolition of a building; or
          (b) any such planning permission has been granted;

the Secretary of State may, on the application of any person, issue a certificate stating that he does not intend to list the building.

(2)    The issue of such a certificate in respect of a building shall –
          (a) preclude the Secretary of State for a period of 5 years from the date of issue from exercising in relation to that building any of the powers conferred on him by Section1; and
          (b) preclude the local planning authority for that period from serving a building preservation notice in relation to it.

(3) Notice of an application under sub-section(1) shall be given to the local planning authority within whose area the building is situated at the same time as the application is submitted to the Secretary of State.

(4) In this section"local planning authority, "in relation to a building in Greater London, includes the Commission.

# 7. Restriction on works affecting listed buildings

Subject to the following provisions of this Act, no person shall execute or cause to be executed any works for the demolition of a listed building or for its alteration or extension in any manner which would affect its character as a building of special architectural or historic interest, unless the works are authorised.

# 9. Offences

(1)    If a person contravenes section 7 he shall be guilty of an offence.

(2)    Without prejudice to sub-section(1), if a person executing or causing to be executed any works in relation to a listed building under a listed building consent fails to comply with any condition attached to the consent, he shall be guilty of an offence.

(3)    In proceedings for an offence under this sectionit shall be a defence to prove the following matters –

(a) that works to the building were urgently necessary in the interests of safety or health or for the preservation of the building;

(b) that it was not practicable to secure safety or health or, as the case may be, the preservation of the building by works of repair or works for affording temporary support or shelter;

(c) that the works carried out were limited to the minimum measures immediately necessary; and

(d) that notice in writing justifying in detail the carrying out of the works was given to the local planning authority as soon as reasonably practicable.

(4)    A person who is guilty of an offence under this sectionshall be liable –

(a)on summary conviction to imprisonment for a term not exceeding six months or fine not exceeding £20,000.00, or both; or

(b) on conviction on indictment to imprisonment for a term not exceeding two years or a fine, or both.

(5)    In determining the amount of any fine to be imposed on a person convicted of an offence under this sectionthe court shall in particular have regard to any financial benefit which has accrued or appears likely to accrue to him in consequence of the offence.

# 66. General duty as respects listed buildings in exercise of planning functions

(1)  In considering whether to grant planning permission for development which affects a listed building or its setting, the local planning authority or, as the case may be, the Secretary of State shall have special regard to the desirability of preserving the building or its setting or any features of special architectural or historic interest which it possesses.

(2)  Without prejudice to section 72 [*General duty as respects conservation areas in exercise of planning functions*], in the exercise of the powers of appropriation, disposal and development (including redevelopment) conferred by the provisions of sections 232, 233 and 235(1) of the principal Act [*i.e. The Town and Country Planning Act 1990*], a local authority shall have regard to the desirability of preserving features of special architectural or historic interest and in particular, listed buildings.

(3)  The reference in sub-section (2) to a local authority includes a reference to a joint planning board.

# 69. Designation of Conservation Areas

(1)  Every local planning authority –
(a) shall from time to time determine which parts of their area are areas of special architectural or historic interest the character or appearance of which it is desirable to preserve or enhance, and
(b) shall designate those areas as conservation areas.

(2)  It shall be the duty of the local planning authority from time to time to review the past exercise of functions under this sectionand to determine whether any parts or any further parts of the area should be designated as conservation areas; and   if they so determine, they shall designate those parts accordingly.

(3)  The Secretary of State may from time to time determine any part of a local planning authority's area which is not for the time being designated as a conservation area is an area of special architectural or historic interest the character of which it is desirable to preserve or enhance; and, if he so determines, he may designate that part as a conservation area.

(4)  The designation of any area as a conservation area shall be a local land charge.

## 70. Designation of Conservation Areas: Supplementary Provisions

(1) The functions of a local planning authority under section 69 and this sectionshall also be exercisable in Greater London by the Commission [*English Heritage*].

(2) Before making a determination under section 69 the Commission shall consult with the Council of each London Borough in which any part is included in the area to which the proposed determination relates.

(3) Before making a determination under section 69(3) the Secretary of State shall consult the local planning authority.

(4) Before designating any area in Greater London as a conservation area the Commission shall obtain the consent of the Secretary of State.

(5) A local planning authority shall give notice of the designation of any part of their area as a conservation area under section 69(1) or (2) and any variation or cancellation of any such designation –

   (a) to the Secretary of State; and
   (b) if it affects an area in England and the designation or, as the case may be the variation or cancellation was not made by the Commission, to the Commission.

(6) The Secretary of State shall give notice of the designation of any part of the area of a local planning authority as a conservation area under section 69(3) and of any variation or cancellation of any such designation–

   (a) to the authority; and
   (b) if it affects an area in England, to the Commission.

(7) A notice under sub-section (5) or (6) shall contain sufficient particulars to identify the area affected.

(8) Notice of any such designation, variation or cancellation as is mentioned in sub-section(5) or (6), with particulars of its effect, shall be published in the London Gazette and in at least one newspaper circulating in the area of the local planning authority, by that authority or, as the case may be, the Secretary of State.

## 71. Formulation and publication of proposals for preservation and enhancement of Conservation Areas

(1) It shall be the duty of a local planning authority from time to time to formulate and publish proposals for the preservation and enhancement of any parts of their area which are conservation areas.

(2) Proposals under this sectionshall be submitted for consideration to a

public meeting in the area to which they relate.

(3)    The local planning authority shall have regard to any views concerning the proposals expressed by persons attending the meeting.

## 72. General duty as respects conservation areas in exercise of planning functions

(1)    In the exercise, with respect to any buildings or other land in a conservation area, of any functions under or by virtue of any of the provisions mentioned in sub-section (2), special attention shall be paid to the desirability of preserving or enhancing the character or appearance of that area.

(2)    The provisions referred to in sub-section(1) are the planning Acts and Part I of the Historic Buildings and Ancient Monuments Act 1953 and sections 70 and 73 of the Leasehold Reform, Housing and Urban Development Act 1993.

## 74. Control of demolition in conservation areas

(1)    A building in a conservation area shall not be demolished without the consent of the appropriate authority (in this Act referred to as "conservation area consent").

(2)    The appropriate authority for the purpose of this sectionis:-
        (a) in relation to applications for consent made by local planning authorities, Secretary of State; and
        (b)in relation to other applications for consent, the local planning authority or the Secretary of State.

(3)    Sections 7 to 26 *[Authorisation of works affecting listed buildings]*, 28 *[Compensation where listed building consent revoked or modified]*, 32 to 46 *[Listed building purchase notices and listed building enforcement notices]*, 56 *[Dangerous structure orders in respect of listed buildings]*, 62 to 65 *[Validity of instruments, decisions and proceedings]*, 66(1) *[General duty as respects listed buildings in exercise of planning functions]*, 82(2) to (4) *[Provisions relating to land and works of local planning authorities]*, 83(1)(b), (3) and (4) *[Crown Land Provisions]* and 90(2) to (4) *[Financial Provisions]* have effect in relation to buildings in conservation areas as they have effect in relation to listed buildings subject to such exceptions and modifications as may be prescribed by regulations.

(4)     Any such regulations may make different provision:-
        (a) in relation to applications made by local planning authorities; and
        (b)   in relation to other applications.

# 75. Cases in which section 74 does not apply

(1)     Section74 does not apply to:–
        (a) listed buildings
        (b) ecclesiastical buildings which are for the time being used for ecclesiastical purposes;
        (c) buildings for the time being included in the schedule of monuments compiled and maintained under Section1 of the Ancient Monuments and Archaeological Areas Act 1979;
        (d) buildings in relation to which a direction under sub-section (2)
is          for the time being in force.

(2)     The Secretary of State may direct that section 74 shall not apply to any description of buildings specified in the direction.

(3)     A direction under sub-section (2) may be given either to an individual local planning authority exercising functions under that sectionor to local planning authorities generally.

(4)     The Secretary of State may vary or revoke a direction under sub-section (2) by a further direction under that sub-section.

(5)     For the purposes of sub-section (1)(b) a building used or available for use by a minister of religion wholly or as mainly as a residence from which to perform the duties of his office shall be treated as not being an ecclesiastical building.

(6)     For the purposes of sections 7 to 9 as they apply by virtue of section 74(3) a building shall be taken to be used for the time being for ecclesiastical purposes if it would be so used but for the works in question.

(7)     The Secretary of State may by order provide for restricting or excluding the operation of sub-section (1)(b) in such cases as may be specified in the order.

(8)     An order under sub-section (7) may:–
        (a)make provisions for buildings generally, for descriptions of buildings or for particular buildings;
        (b) make different provisions for buildings in different areas, for buildings of different religious faiths or denominations or according to the use made of the building;
        (c) make such provision in relation to a part of a building (including, in particular, an object or structure falling to be treated as part of the building by virtue of section 1(5) as may be made in relation to a building and make different provision for different

parts of the same building;

(d) make different provision with respect to works of different descriptions or according to the extent of the works;

(e) make such consequential adaptations or modifications of the operation of any other provision of this Act or the Principal Act, or of any instrument made under either of those Acts as appear to the Secretary of State to be appropriate.

(9)   Regulations under this Act may provide that sub-sections (5) to (8) shall have effect subject to such exceptions or modifications and may be described and any such regulations may make different provision–

(a) in relation to applications made by local planning authorities and

(b) in relation to other applications.

(10)   Any proceedings on or arising out of an application for conservation area consent made while section 74 applies to a building shall lapse if it ceases to apply to it and any such consent granted with respect to the building shall also lapse.

(11)   The fact that that sectionhas ceased to apply to a building shall not affect the liability of any person to be prosecuted and punished for an offence under section 9 or 43 committed with respect to the building that section did apply to it.

# · Index ·